Frommer's

MEMORABLE WALKS IN LONDON

6th Edition

Richard Jones

WILEY

Wiley Publishing, Inc.

Published by:

WILEY PUBLISHING, INC.

111 River St.
Hoboken, NJ 07030-5774

ISBN-13: 978-0-471-77338-2
ISBN-10: 0-471-77338-7

Editor: Elizabeth Albertson
Production Editor: Jana M. Stefanciosa
Photo Editor: Richard Fox
Cartographer: Anton Crane
Production by Wiley Indianapolis Composition Services

For information on our other products and services or to obtain technical support, please contact our Customer Care Department within the U.S. at 800/762-2974, outside the U.S. at 317/572-3993 or fax 317/572-4002.

Wiley also publishes its books in a variety of electronic formats. Some content that appears in print may not be available in electronic formats.

Manufactured in the United States of America

5   4   3   2   1

Contents

LIST OF MAPS

The Walking Tours

• • • • • • • • • • • • • • • •

About the Author

Londoner **Richard Jones** has been devising walking tours of his city since 1982. He has also written and presented drama documentaries about Shakespeare in London (1999) and Jack the Ripper (1997).

An Invitation to the Reader

In researching this book, we discovered many wonderful places—hotels, restaurants, shops, and more. We're sure you'll find others. Please tell us about them, so we can share the information with your fellow travelers in upcoming editions. If you were disappointed with a recommendation, we'd love to know that, too. Please write to:

Frommer's Memorable Walks in London, 6th Edition
Wiley Publishing, Inc.
111 River St. • Hoboken, NJ 07030-5774

An Additional Note

Please be advised that travel information is subject to change at any time—and this is especially true of prices. We therefore suggest that you write or call ahead for confirmation when making your travel plans. The authors, editors, and publisher cannot be held responsible for the experiences of readers while traveling. Your safety is important to us, however, so we encourage you to stay alert and be aware of your surroundings. Keep a close eye on cameras, purses, and wallets, all favorite targets of thieves and pickpockets.

Frommers.com

Now that you have the guidebook to a great trip, visit our website at **www.frommers.com** for travel information on more than 3,000 destinations. With features updated regularly, we give you instant access to the most current trip-planning information available. You'll find the best prices on airfares, accommodations, and car rentals—and you can even book travel online through our travel booking partners. At Frommers.com, you'll also find the following:

- Online updates to our most popular guidebooks
- Vacation sweepstakes and contest giveaways
- Newsletter highlighting the hottest travel trends
- Online travel message boards with featured travel discussions

Introducing the City by the Thames

Sprawling across 1,600-plus sq. km (600-plus sq. miles) and housing eight million residents, greater London has been building, growing, and changing continuously for almost 2,000 years. The city's commercial core, the West End, is laid out with broad boulevards and huge palaces, reflecting the city's former status as the capital of a globe-spanning empire. When you leave the West End, however, you'll immediately note how diverse London has become. The centuries have shaped it into a complex amalgam of communities—a collection of towns, each with its own tradition and spirit.

The mix of cultures—a relic of what was once known as the British Empire—gives London a certain depth of character that has long kept it at the forefront of the world's art, music, and fashion scenes. The ever-changing myriad of immigrant communities has constantly challenged and redefined London's character. Though less important than it once was, the British class system stubbornly endures. Royal London's pomp and

The Tours at a Glance

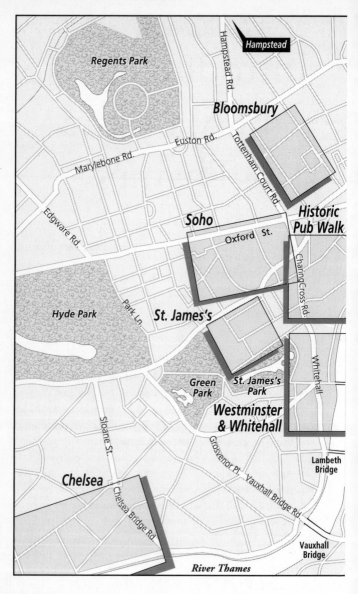

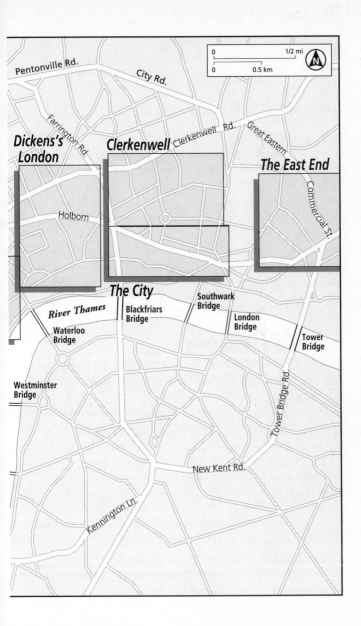

Dickens's London

Clerkenwell

The East End

Pentonville Rd.

City Rd.

Farrington Rd.

Clerkenwell Rd.

Great Eastern

Commercial St.

Holborn

The City

River Thames

Blackfriars
Bridge

Southwark
Bridge

London
Bridge

Tower
Bridge

Waterloo
Bridge

Westminster
Bridge

Tower Bridge Rd.

New Kent Rd.

Kennington Ln.

0   1/2 mi
0   0.5 km

N

pageantry might look increasingly like a tourist attraction, but daily ceremonies such as the Changing of the Guard and the Ceremony of the Keys are striking reminders of an influential cultural heritage. Ironically, the scandal-ridden Royal Family appears to be symbolic of the nation's troubles.

The eleven walking tours in this book are organized by either geographical area or topic. They'll take you off the main streets as much as possible—they'll lead you down unexpected passages and into secluded courtyards; introduce you to that most English of institutions, the pub; guide you through the streets of Dickens's London to show you the landmarks he might still recognize; and help you discover, all over the city, sights and corners you might not have found by yourself.

The approximate time that each tour should take is specified. None of the walks are physically strenuous—each is designed to be accessible (and interesting) to all ages. Walk, look, listen, learn, and enjoy. And if you get hungry, see our suggestions for Best Dining Bets on p. 170.

LONDON'S BEGINNINGS

Though scholars debate the origin of London's name, popular belief is that it comes from the Celtic *Llyn Din,* meaning "lakeside fortress."

When the Romans arrived, they chose Londinium as the name for their settlement on the Thames. They built a bridge, and the town began to flourish around the north bank of the bridgehead. In the late 2nd century, the Romans erected a massive wall of Kentish ragstone around the city to protect it from attack by neighboring tribes (you can still see remnants of the wall; see Walking Tour 1). Within a century, the population increased to 15,000, and Londinium became a bustling center of trade and industry. Roman Britain lasted until the 5th century, when Saxon invaders began to encroach on southern England. Meanwhile, Rome itself came under siege, and in A.D. 410 Londinium's Roman troops departed for home.

Over the next 400 years, various Germanic tribes, collectively called Anglo-Saxons, began to settle in England; by A.D. 871, they were united under Alfred the Great, the first in a line of Saxon kings. He strengthened London's fortifications against the Vikings, whose raids were a constant threat. Later, Edward the Confessor (1003–66), who was to be canonized, transferred the court and government from Winchester to Westminster. He rebuilt Westminster Abbey, and Harold II, the last of the Saxon rulers, was crowned there.

However, it was William the Conqueror who first understood the political importance of London. He left an indelible mark on the city, and his 1066 coronation in Westminster Abbey established a precedent that has been followed ever since. He recognized London as the country's capital and allowed the City of London to continue electing its own leaders—a decision that was to have far-reaching consequences. English monarchs from that time on, eager for the support of the wealthy merchants of the city, strove to hold London as the key to controlling England. William also built the White Tower, which was later incorporated into the Tower of London.

By the 15th century, the banks of the Thames were lined with warehouses and great mansions built by the rising merchants. The population had grown to 30,000, and ecclesiastical establishments were flourishing (their names—Whitefriars, Blackfriars, Greyfriars—still remain part of London). The suburbs expanded beyond the city's walls, and many new ones were created; however, because there was no central planning, the roads developed haphazardly, creating the confusing street patterns that still exist today.

TUDORS & STUARTS, PLAGUE & FIRE

Modern London began with the Tudors. Henry VIII built St. James's Palace and enclosed what is now Hyde Park and Green Park for his private grounds. When Henry broke with Rome, introducing the English Reformation, his dissolution of the monasteries led to the destruction of many of London's medieval ecclesiastical buildings. The church's wealth was confiscated and redistributed to a new aristocracy that supported the monarch; among those who were executed for refusing to acknowledge Henry's supremacy as head of the church was the internationally prominent man of letters Sir Thomas More, author of *Utopia*.

The ascension of Elizabeth I ushered in an era of peace and prosperity. Elizabethan England was a period of unparalleled creativity. Poetry, theater, and spectacle flourished. Open-air playhouses, including Shakespeare's Globe Theatre, were built in the borough of Southwark (the city fathers had puritanically banned theaters in the belief that they attracted the wrong element). Plays by Shakespeare, Ben Jonson, and Christopher Marlowe were performed there. Today, London's recently reconstructed Globe Theater on the south bank of the Thames continues this tradition.

Along with the flowering of the arts, England entered a period of colonial and mercantile expansion in rivalry with Spain, and London was a prime beneficiary. All these trends continued after the defeat of the Spanish Armada and lasted into the Jacobean period, after James I took the throne. John Donne's poetry and John Webster's tragic dramas built upon literary and dramatic traditions. Inigo Jones (1573–1652), generally viewed as the first modern British architect, introduced Palladian style into London and built the Queen's House at Greenwich and the Banqueting House at Whitehall.

During this time, however, the conflict that had developed between the Stuart kings and the Puritans steadily intensified. Religion was not the only issue. Crucial was the king's claim to the privileges of a divine-right monarch in opposition to a parliament that advocated constitutional monarchy. After the Puritan victory in 1649, Charles I stepped through the window of the Banqueting Hall and onto the scaffold, where he lost his head.

In the years that followed, the arts were rigorously suppressed, and many of the important Gothic cathedrals were damaged—stained glass was smashed and religious artifacts were destroyed. Though the great poet John Milton supported the Puritans, he published his most noted works, *Paradise Lost* and *Samson Agonistes,* after the restoration of Charles II in 1660.

Although plague had long been endemic in London, it didn't attain epidemic proportions until 1665, when tens of thousands died in what became known as "the Great Plague." In the next year, medieval London was destroyed by the Great Fire. Fanned by strong easterly winds, the fire burned more than 10,000 buildings, taking with it the crowded and unsanitary half-timbered buildings that had helped to spread the plague. After the fire, houses were rebuilt of stone and brick. Christopher Wren, who was commissioned to redesign the city, then built his masterpieces: St. Paul's Cathedral and St. Mary-le-Bow, Chelsea Royal Hospital, Kensington Palace, and dozens of other London buildings.

18TH-CENTURY LONDON

In the 18th century, England was transformed into a world-class financial and military power, and London again became the primary beneficiary of the new prosperity. This was the great era of Georgian architecture, which you can still see in Grosvenor, Bedford, and Hanover Squares, as well as in other London squares and streets. The Georgian style spilled over into the applied arts, including furniture, silver, and glass. The great porcelain works and potteries of Wedgwood, Spode, and Staffordshire were established at this time. Two new bridges—Blackfriars and Westminster—were built, streets were upgraded, and hospitals were improved. A number of painters gained prominence, including Joshua Reynolds, Thomas Gainsborough, and William Hogarth; several noteworthy sculptors, including Grinling Gibbons, also emerged. Samuel Johnson compiled his famous dictionary, James Boswell wrote his great biography of the lexicographer/critic, and David Garrick performed his memorable Shakespearean roles at his playhouse in Drury Lane (often changing Shakespeare's tragic endings to happy ones to suit the temper of the times). The new wealth produced by the Industrial Revolution led to the emergence of a middle class that soon partly merged with and bolstered the older, land-owning aristocracy.

VICTORIAN LONDON

Queen Victoria ascended the throne in 1837 and reigned for 64 years, the longest tenure in English history. Because the new middle class believed that education was essential to prosperity, the University of London and free municipal public libraries were established. The National Gallery at Trafalgar Square was completed in 1838, and the British Museum's new building in Bloomsbury was finished in 1857. Progress changed the face of London, transforming it into a modern metropolis as rail lines and steam engines, underground trains, sewage systems, and new building techniques greatly expanded its borders. Buckingham Palace was enlarged and sheathed in honey-colored stone, and the Gothic extravagance of the Albert Memorial defined an architectural style that only recently has begun to be appreciated.

Victorian London was the center of the largest empire the world had ever seen. Londoners traveled all over the globe to fill military and administrative posts. This period is the one that still influences our present-day view of London and of the English: It was shaped by the growing power of the bourgeoisie, the queen's moralistic stance, and the perceived responsibilities of managing an empire. The racy London of the preceding 3 centuries moved underground. Meanwhile, in the poorer neighborhoods, the dialects and attitudes (later referred to as *cockney*) were developing. The cockney humor of London's vaudeville and music halls influenced the entertainment industry from Sydney to San Francisco.

The outbreak of World War I marked the end of an era: Until then, it had been widely assumed that peace, progress, prosperity, empire, and, incidentally, social improvement would continue indefinitely. Following World War I came 2 decades of social unrest and political uncertainty, both at home and throughout the empire.

WORLD WAR II & AFTER

During World War II, London suffered repeated bombings, and almost every notable building was seriously damaged. Trenches were dug in public parks, and the Underground stations doubled as bomb shelters. The heroism and stoicism with which this ordeal was endured is still a source of local pride.

Modern office structures, centrally heated apartment buildings, and successive waves of immigrants have literally and figuratively changed the face of contemporary London. Many tourists are disappointed when they first arrive because the past isn't immediately or easily visible, but if they scratch the surface, they'll find a complex city that's a combination of all the preceding eras.

Since the 12th century, the City of London had been governed by an independent corporation headed by the Lord Mayor, but in 1986, this authority was replaced. Governing responsibility was divided between the central government and the boroughs. However, one of London's most colorful pageants, the Lord Mayor's Procession and Show, derives from the ancient right of the City of London Corporation to require the monarch to ask the Lord Mayor's permission to enter the city's original square mile.

The city's tangle of streets originated as paths during the Middle Ages. Several buildings from the 15th century still stand, including Guildhall (see Walking Tour 1) and Southwark Cathedral. Throughout London you'll find examples of Tudor and Stuart architecture, designed in the English Renaissance style. Banqueting House (see Walking Tour 4), St. Paul's Cathedral (see Walking Tour 1), and the Chelsea Royal Hospital (see Walking Tour 10) are three distinctive examples.

London's past is also present in its street names, although most of the structures they recall are long gone. Bucklesbury and Lothbury refer to the *buhrs* (stone mansions) of Norman barons. Ludgate, Aldgate, and Cripplegate refer to ancient gates of the city wall. The word *Barbican* derives from the watchtower that once stood in its place. In the Middle Ages, *cheaps* were markets—hence, the origin of names such as Eastcheap and Cheapside. Some streets bear the names of products formerly sold there—look for Milk Street, Bread Street, and Friday Street (where fish was sold).

The City

Start: Bank Underground Station.

Finish: St. Paul's Underground Station.

Time: 2½ to 3 hours.

Best Time: Weekdays from 10am to 4pm.

Worst Time: Nights and weekends, when many buildings are closed.

The City of London occupies approximately 2.6 square kilometers (1 sq. mile). It was the Londinium of the Romans, who erected a protective wall around it in the 2nd century A.D. During the Middle Ages, a series of gates was built to facilitate entry into the City; these are now commemorated in street names such as Newgate and Aldersgate (older gate). Other streets in the City are named for the goods and services that were traded there, such as Bread Street, Cloth Fair, Wood Street, and even Love Lane.

In the early Middle Ages, the City asserted its independence from royal jurisdiction; it established an autonomous government with a Lord Mayor and a court of aldermen (elders). Today, the City is England's financial center. It remains an autonomous precinct, creating and enforcing its own laws on certain local matters. Many of the winding, narrow streets have changed little over the centuries, making this part of London one of the most interesting for strolling.

• • • • • • • • • • • • • • • • •

Leave Bank Underground Station via the Royal Exchange exit (Exit 3) and head up the steps to enter:

1. **The Royal Exchange,** founded by Sir Thomas Gresham in the mid–16th century for the purpose of trading wholesale and retail goods. The present building, designed by Sir William Tite, dates from 1844. In 2001, the building was converted into a collection of up-market shops—several designer stores are now found within its historic walls. Once inside, ascend any of the corner stair-cases and walk around the balcony to view the late-19th-century paintings, which grace each one of the wall alcoves and depict important events from the city's past.

Backtrack to the steps of the Royal Exchange and look to your right over Threadneedle Street. The large neoclas-sical building opposite is the:

2. **Bank of England,** designed by Sir John Soane and built between 1788 and 1833, with a new complex added by Sir Herbert Baker between the two World Wars. The bank was established "for the Publick Good and Benefit of Our People" in 1694, when a Royal Charter was granted by William III and Mary II.

Known as "the Old Lady of Threadneedle Street," this is the central bank, managing the public debt and serving as a depository for government funds. It's also the institu-tion that issues bank notes for general circulation.

If you'd like to visit the **Bank of England Museum** (© 020/7601-5545), cross Threadneedle Street, bear right, and take the first left into Bartholomew Lane, where you'll find the museum entrance on the left. The museum is open Monday through Friday 10am to 5pm; admission is free.

Retrace your steps to the front of the Royal Exchange. Cross over Cornhill, where, in the middle of the street, you'll see a statue commemorating J. H. Greathead. Greathead invented the traveling shield, a rotating, drill-like implement that made it possible to excavate the tun-nels of London's Underground system around and under the Thames.

The City

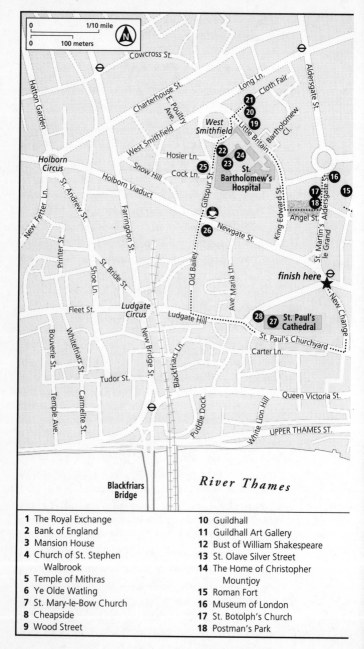

Blackfriars Bridge

River Thames

1 The Royal Exchange
2 Bank of England
3 Mansion House
4 Church of St. Stephen
    Walbrook
5 Temple of Mithras
6 Ye Olde Watling
7 St. Mary-le-Bow Church
8 Cheapside
9 Wood Street

10 Guildhall
11 Guildhall Art Gallery
12 Bust of William Shakespeare
13 St. Olave Silver Street
14 The Home of Christopher
    Mountjoy
15 Roman Fort
16 Museum of London
17 St. Botolph's Church
18 Postman's Park

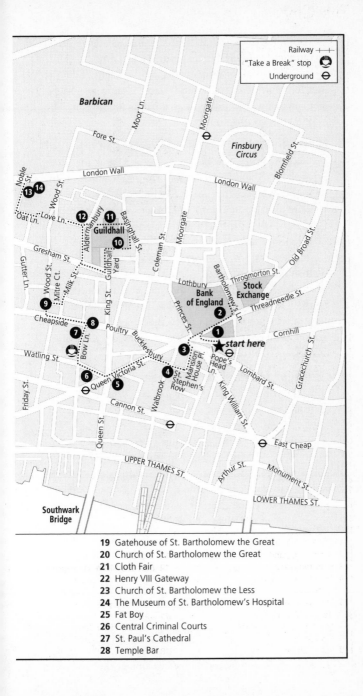

Bear right along Cornhill, and go left when you arrive at the Underground Station exit. Cross Lombard Street via the pedestrian crossing, and then veer right. Take the first left into Mansion House Place. Continue into St. Stephen's Row, and follow it as it bends sharp right. The building on your right is the:

3. **Mansion House,** the official residence of the Lord Mayor. The house was built by George Dance the Elder between 1739 and 1753. The Corinthian columns form an impressive backdrop for the Lord Mayor's appearance at ceremonial functions. The main reception room, Egyptian Hall, is the setting for official banquets. Alas, Mansion House is closed to the public.

At the end of St. Stephen's Row, turn left into **Walbrook.** This street is named for the brook around which the Romans built their original London settlement. By the 14th century, the brook had become polluted and work was begun to cover it over. By the 16th century, no further trace of it remained. Immediately on your left is the entrance to the:

4. **Church of St. Stephen Walbrook.** This might be not only the finest church designed by Wren, but also London's most beautiful church. *The Critical Review of Publick Buildings in London* (1734) observed that it was "famous all over Europe and justly reputed the master-piece of the celebrated Sir Christopher Wren. Perhaps Italy itself can produce no modern buildings that can vie with this in taste or proportion."

The **altar,** at the church's center, was carved by Henry Moore. When the rector, Chad Varah (who founded the Samaritans in the 1950s), asked the sculptor to create an altar, Moore replied that he was an agnostic. Chad respond-ed, "Henry, I'm not asking you to take the service. I under-stand that you're a bit of a chiseler; just do your job."

Exit the church, cross Walbrook, and proceed into Bucklesbury. Walk straight ahead and bear left into Queen Victoria Street. One block farther, turn left and go up the steps outside the main entrance of Temple Court. Turn left and stop by the railings to look at the:

5. **Temple of Mithras,** Queen Victoria Street. The temple
was discovered in 1954, when developers were excavating
a new building site. Mithraism, an ancient Persian cult
introduced to London by Roman soldiers, became widely
accepted during the 2nd century. The temple was built in
the 3rd century, when the religion was at the height of its
popularity. The temple was most likely destroyed in the
4th century, when the Roman Empire under Constantine
accepted Christianity (many pagan temples were torn
down at that time). The temple's former entrance is to
your right, at the end of the central nave (lined with
columns dividing it into aisles). Sculptures and other
objects from the temple are now on display at the
Museum of London.

Return to the top of the steps outside Temple Court;
looking left, you'll have a great view of St. Paul's Cathedral.
Cross Queen Victoria Street and make your way to the red
telephone box on Watling Street. Proceed along Watling
for half a block; on your left, you'll come to:

6. **Ye Olde Watling,** 29 Watling St. (no phone). Sir
Christopher Wren constructed this building in 1668 to
house the workmen who were rebuilding St. Paul's
Cathedral after the devastation caused by the Great Fire of
London (1666). Wood from dismantled sailing ships
makes up the structure of this atmospheric old pub. Good
lunches are available here, as are Bass, IPA, Best Bitter,
and other beers. You can stop for a break here or wait for
the next stop.

Cross Watling Street onto **Bow Lane,** a charming little pedestrian thoroughfare that evokes the medieval period. Before the 16th century, this lane was called
Cordwainers Street, named for the shoemakers and
leather workers who lived and traded here. It was renamed
for the nearby church of St. Mary-Le-Bow.

A few steps down Bow Lane, turn left into covered
Groveland Court to find:

Take a Break **Williamson's Tavern** (© 020/ 7248-5750). In the 17th century, this was the site of the official residence of the Lord Mayor of the City of London. The wrought-iron gates in front were presented to the Lord Mayor by William III (1650–1702) and Mary II (1662–94). Inside, you'll see a fireplace made of ancient Roman tiles that were discovered on this site when the pub was erected. The tavern is famous with locals for its terrific steak sandwiches.

Retrace your footsteps to Bow Lane and turn left. After another half block, turn left into Bow Churchyard. Turn right into the main churchyard, and then right again through the gates to descend into the crypt of:

7. **St. Mary-le-Bow Church.** In the crypt, you'll find the remains of previous churches that formerly existed on this site, as well as the arches (also known as "bows") for which Bow Lane was named.

Exit the crypt and turn right into Bow Churchyard. To the left you'll see a **statue of Capt. John Smith,** a parishioner of St. Mary-le-Bow and one of the first colonists to settle Jamestown, Virginia. The early survival of this first permanent English settlement in North America might well have been due to Smith's leadership and ability to adapt to the new environment.

A little farther along on the right is the church entrance. Traditionally, an authentic cockney was defined as someone born within hearing range of the Bow bells. The first mention of this church was in 1091, when it was recorded that the roof blew off in a storm—the beginning of what seemed to be a string of bad luck. In 1196, William Fitz Osbert was smoked out of the church's tower after murdering one of the Archbishop of Canterbury's guards. In 1271, the tower fell, killing 20 people. In 1284, a local goldsmith was murdered in the church. In 1331, Queen Phillipa (wife of Edward III) and several of her attendants were injured when a balcony collapsed. Finally, the church was destroyed in the Great Fire of 1666. The present building, rebuilt by Wren, was modeled after Rome's Church of the Basilica of Maxentius. The 66m (217-ft.) steeple is widely considered Wren's finest. Inside, look at the arches flanking the nave: each is topped by a stone relief of a World War II allied head of state, including Winston Churchill, Charles de Gaulle, and Franklin D. Roosevelt.

Turn left into the street in front of the church. This is:

8. **Cheapside,** formerly one of London's busiest commercial streets. From the 13th to the 17th centuries, this thoroughfare was a bustling marketplace for jewelry, shoes, bread, meat, spices, wine, and all sorts of other trinkets and supplies. Its name derives from the Anglo-Saxon word *ceap* (or *chepe*), meaning "to barter." This is the origin of the modern word *cheap,* and *shopping* evolved from the word *cheping.*

Cheapside's timber-frame shops were destroyed by the Great Fire, after which the street was widened and lined with higher buildings. The expansion of London in the late 18th and 19th centuries gave rise to a rival area—Oxford Street, which is now one of the city's most important shopping streets.

Cautiously cross Cheapside and continue to the left. One block ahead, turn right into:

9. **Wood Street,** London's former timber-selling center. Look up at the large plane tree on your left at the corner of Cheapside. This tree was immortalized by the Romantic poet William Wordsworth in "The Reverie of Poor Susan":

> *At the corner of Wood Street*
> *when daylight appears*
> *Hangs a thrush that sings loud,*
> *It has sung for three years.*
> *Poor Susan has passed by the spot,*
> *and has heard*
> *In the silence of morning,*
> *the song of the bird.*

Take the first right turn into Milk Street and follow it around to the left. Proceed ahead and turn right into Gresham Street. Cross the street and make your way to the Church of St. Lawrence Jewry. Turn left by the church and proceed into the courtyard of:

10. **Guildhall** (☎ 020/7606-3030), the City of London's City Hall and the seat of the Lord Mayor and the Court of Aldermen since the 12th century. The present building was completed in 1439 but was severely damaged in the Great Fire and again by German bombers in December 1940.

    Once inside the hall, look back at the entrance door. On the right side is **Gog** and on the left is **Magog.** According to legend, these two ferocious-looking giants represent warriors in the conflict between the ancient inhabitants of Britain and Trojan invaders. The outcome of this conflict was the establishment of New Troy, reputedly on the site of present-day London. With your back to the giants, look left to the **statue of Winston Churchill,** unveiled on June 21, 1955.

    At the far end of the hall, beside the doorway on the left, is a board listing some of the trials that have taken place here. Included is the name of **Dr. Roderigo Lopez,** a Portuguese Jew who served as physician to Elizabeth I. He was accused of (and later executed for) trying to poison the queen. As one of the most despised citizens of his day, Lopez might have been the model for Shylock in Shakespeare's *The Merchant of Venice.*

    Exit Guildhall and turn left to visit:

11. **Guildhall Art Gallery** (☎ 020/7332-3700; www.guildhall-art-gallery.org.uk), originally established in 1885 to house and display paintings and sculpture belonging to the corporation of London. The original art gallery was destroyed during World War II; the modern state-of-the-art structure that stands alongside the historic Guildhall was designed by Richard Gilbert Scott and opened to the public in 1999. The collection includes a number of famous pre-Raphaelite works, as well as John Singleton Copley's ***Defeat of the Floating Batteries at Gibraltar,*** one of Britain's largest oil paintings. The gallery is open Monday to Saturday 10am to 5pm and Sunday from noon to 4pm. There is an admission charge.

    During construction of the gallery, the remnants of the eastern entrance to a Roman amphitheater were discovered. It was long believed that Londinium would have possessed an amphitheater, but it was only in 1988 that

Museum of London archaeologists discovered the remains during excavations. So important was the discovery that the building's designs were revised so that the relics could remain exactly where they had been found. Today they are preserved beneath the art gallery, where they can be viewed during a visit.

Exit Guildhall Art Gallery and go straight across the courtyard, where you'll find the entrance to the **Guildhall Library.** Open Monday to Saturday from 9:30am to 5pm, the library contains excellent source material on London history. This is also the entrance to the **Clock Museum,** which displays antique clocks loaned by the Worshipful Company of Clockmakers. The Clock Museum is open Monday through Saturday 9:30am to 4:30pm; admission is free.

Pass under the offices to the left of the library entrance and bear right along Aldermanbury. When you've reached the end of Aldermanbury, cross over Love Lane to the garden, where you can see a:

12. **Bust of William Shakespeare** commemorating John Heminge and Henry Condell—fellow actors and personal friends of Shakespeare who lived for many years in this parish. Heminge and Condell collected all of Shakespeare's known works and arranged for the publication of the first folio of his plays in 1623. As inscribed on the monument: "They thus merited the gratitude of mankind." Behind the bust are the remains of the **Church of St. Mary Aldermanbury,** which was dismantled in the 1960s and reassembled at Westminster College in Fulton, Missouri, as a memorial to Winston Churchill.

Continue along **Love Lane,** once a notorious red-light district that was named for the services dispensed there. Cross Wood Street and proceed into the covered passageway called St. Alban's Court, bearing left and then right into Oat Lane and, a block later, right onto Noble Street. At the end of the block is a small garden, with the remains of a church called:

13. **St. Olave Silver Street.** Go up the steps and follow the pathway. Pause at the top of the next set of steps and look at the vast modern office block that stands on what is

possibly one of London's most interesting literary sites, for here once stood:

14. **The Home of Christopher Mountjoy.** A Frenchman, Mountjoy made wigs and fashionable headdresses. He lived at the corner of the former Silver and Monkwell streets with his wife, his daughter, an apprentice named Stephen Bellott, and a lodger named William Shakespeare. The parents wanted their daughter, Mary, to marry the apprentice, and Mme. Mountjoy persuaded Shakespeare to act as matchmaker. He was successful, and the marriage took place at the Church of St. Olave Silver Street on November 19, 1604. Mme. Mountjoy died a few years later, and a dispute arose between Stephen Bellott and his father-in-law. In 1612, Bellott brought suit against Mountjoy in the Court of Requests; one of the witnesses summoned to give evidence was Shakespeare. From his evidence and the testimony of other witnesses, we know that Shakespeare lived with the Mountjoys for 6 years before the wedding and probably several more afterward. It is believed that Shakespeare wrote ten plays while living here.

Retrace your footsteps to Noble Street. Cross over to the building marked **1 London Wall** to look at some of the remains of the city wall. The wall is of Roman origin up to a height of about 2.4m (8 ft.); the remainder was added during the medieval period.

Facing the wall, walk left along Noble Street; at the end of the railings, look down at the remains of the:

15. **Roman Fort,** one of London's oldest structures. Built around A.D. 120, the fort originally covered 4.9 hectares (12 acres) and accommodated the guards of the Roman Governor of Britain. At least 1,000 men were housed in the barracks. These remaining walls were part of the curved southwest-corner watchtower.

Continue to the end of Noble Street and turn right onto Gresham Street. One block later, turn right and continue to the pedestrian crossing; cross Aldersgate Street. To the right is the:

16. **Museum of London** (© 020/7600-3699), which houses artifacts excavated along much of this walk. It's

open Tuesday to Saturday from 10am to 5:50pm and Sunday from noon to 5:50pm. Admission is free.

Ahead of you on Aldersgate Street is:

17. **St. Botolph's Church** (© 020/7606-0684), one of three city churches dedicated to the patron saint of travelers. All three stand near the former site of a city gate—in this case, Aldersgate. If the church is open, you can explore its interesting interior, featuring a splendid barrel-vaulted roof and a sword rest for the Lord Mayor's sword of state.

Walk through the gate to the left of the church to enter:

18. **Postman's Park,** named for its former proximity to the General Post Office. Walk straight ahead to the small monument with the red terra-cotta roof. This is the Heroes' Wall, a national memorial commemorating acts of heroism by ordinary men and women. Dedicated in 1910, the wall is covered with epitaphs to unsung heroes such as John Cranmer, age 23, who "drowned off Ostend whilst saving the life of a stranger and a foreigner." The wall and park were used as a location in the film *Bridget Jones: The Edge of Reason.*

Continue through the park and exit via the gate opposite the one you entered through. Turn right onto Little Britain, cross at the pedestrian crossing, and continue right to follow its course. At the end, on the right, is the:

19. **Gatehouse of St. Bartholomew the Great,** at Smithfield Square. Take a step back to admire this picturesque structure. Above the gate is one of the earliest surviving timber-frame house fronts in London. It was built by William Scudamore in 1595 and restored in 1916 after damage from a zeppelin bomb. Parts of the stone gate date from 1240, though most of the stonework was installed during a restoration in 1932.

Walk through the gatehouse and straight into the:

20. **Church of St. Bartholomew the Great,** London's oldest parish church, which is part of an Augustinian priory founded in 1123 by a monk named Rahere. The church was spared in the Great Fire and during the World War II bombings. You might feel that there's something

familiar about this church—it has frequently been featured in films, including *Shakespeare in Love, Robin Hood: Prince of Thieves,* and *Four Weddings and a Funeral.*

Just inside the door, on your right, are the church's 15th-century cloisters. Walk along the right aisle of the church, pause by the second radiator on your right, and look up at the **monument to Edward Cooke,** a philosopher and Doctor of Physick who died in 1652. The marble from which the statue is made condenses water from the air in wet weather—thus, it "weeps." (The inscription asks you to watch for this.)

Go to the central aisle and face the main altar. To the left is the **tomb of Rahere.** Rahere was a courtier at the court of Henry I, but when the heir to the throne drowned at sea, Rahere became a monk. Later, on a pilgrimage to Rome, he came down with malaria. He vowed that if God cured him, he'd return to London and build a church. After Rahere recovered from his illness, he returned home to fulfill his vow; he supposedly chose the spot after a dream in which St. Bartholomew told him to go to "the smoothfield without the city gates and build there a church, hospital, and monastery."

With your back to the main altar, look up to your left at the lovely oriel window, called **Prior Bolton's Window.** As prior from 1506 to 1532, Bolton had his quarters behind this window, which he had constructed so that he could watch the monks at their service. Beneath the central pane is his rebus—a pictorial representation of his name—dating from a time when most people could neither read nor write. This one depicts a crossbow bolt piercing a wine barrel, or tun, so that parishioners would read the picture as "Bolt tun."

Cross to the far aisle and turn left. Pause by the second window on the right. To the left of two enormous jugs is the **monument to John and Margaret Whiting,** a couple who died within a year of each other. The inscription ends with these lines:

> *Shee first deceased, hee for a little Tryd*
> *To live without her, Liked it not and dyd.*

In 1539, Henry VIII confiscated all of this church's property; it was then used for stables, as a private home, and as a printing office where Benjamin Franklin worked in 1725. The church is open Sunday from 8am to 1pm and 2 to 8pm and Monday to Friday from 8:30am to 5:30pm. It's closed Mondays in August.

Backtrack through the timbered gatehouse, turn right, and then take the first right into:

21. **Cloth Fair,** site of the Bartholomew Fair, a sort of medieval street carnival held annually from 1123 to 1855. Turn left into Cloth Court, where the gabled houses on the right date from 1604 and are among the few examples of buildings that predate the Great Fire.

Look up at the wall opposite, where you'll see the **Sailors Homecoming Window.** To the right of this is a blue plaque commemorating the fact that Sir John Betjeman (1906–84), a Poet Laureate, lived here.

Backtrack along Cloth Fair and turn left into West Smithfield. To your right is **Smithfield Market** (see stop 4 in Walking Tour 7, p. 103). Follow the road as it bears right. A little way along, pause by the **William Wallace Memorial.** It was here, on what was then known as the *smooth field,* that Sir William Wallace ("Braveheart") was hanged, drawn, and quartered on August 23, 1305.

As you continue along West Smithfield, notice that the wall on your left is somewhat pockmarked. This damage was caused by shrapnel when a zeppelin dropped a bomb on the square in 1916. Farther along, on the left, is the:

22. **Henry VIII Gateway,** built free of charge in 1702 by the stonemasons who constructed St. Paul's Cathedral. Above it is the only outdoor statue of Henry VIII in London, commemorating the king's donation of the hospital to the City of London following his dissolution of the monasteries.

Go through the gateway a little distance; on the left you'll come to the entrance to the:

23. **Church of St. Bartholomew the Less.** Located on this site since 1184, this is the official church of St. Bartholomew's Hospital. Note the two 15th-century arches that survive under the tower. Go up the steps to your left; just in front of the wooden screen, pull back the green carpet to see the 14th-century memorial to William

and Alice Markeby. When you leave, be sure to replace the carpet over the brass.

Exit left from the church and pass under the arch. On the left you'll find:

24. **The Museum of St. Bartholomew's Hospital** (**(℡ 020/7601-8033**). St. Bartholomew's is London's oldest hospital still standing on its original site. The museum displays a range of artifacts that illustrate the hospital's colorful and fascinating history. The magnificent staircase in the Great Hall, which can be viewed from the museum, is hung with two large paintings by William Hogarth (1697–1764), *The Pool and Bethesda* and *The Good Samaritan.* It is said that Hogarth used patients from the hospital as his models, and such was his eye for detail that modern doctors can still look at the subjects and diagnose the diseases from which they were suffering! The museum is open Monday to Friday from 10am to 4pm; admission is free.

Retrace your footsteps to the main gate. Turn left into Giltspur Street. One block down, on the right and above the corner of Cock Lane, is the:

25. **Fat Boy** (or Golden Boy), erected by the City of London together with a plaque that reads: "This boy is in memory put up for the late Fire of London, occasion'd by the sin of gluttony 1666." Popular myth holds that the Great Fire was God's way of punishing overindulgent Londoners.

Continue 1 block to the end of Giltspur Street. Note on the right the **Church of the Holy Sepulchre.** Founded in 1137 just outside the city wall's northern gate, this was the departure point for the knights of the Crusades. It was named after the Holy Sepulchre Church in Jerusalem, the Crusaders' destination. The present building dates from 1450.

At the intersection of Giltspur and Newgate Streets is the:

Take a Break **Viaduct Tavern,** 126 Newgate St. (no phone). Built in 1875, this is the City of London's only remaining example of a late-19th-century "gin palace." The pub's copper ceiling and painted oils on canvas were intended to attract customers from their ordinary dwellings to this spectacular "palace." When the pub was refurbished in 1994, one of its original mirrors was found—you can see it along the staircase leading to the restrooms. In addition to Tetley and Pedigree bitters, the pub offers "guest" ales that change weekly. You can also order toasted sandwiches, sausages, baked potatoes, and the like.

Directly across from the pub are the:

26. **Central Criminal Courts.** These courts are better known as the world-famous Old Bailey (where John Mortimer's well-known character, barrister Horace Rumpole, had many a legal skirmish), named after the street in which they stand. The building occupies the site of the former Newgate Prison, which was demolished in 1902. Inside, you can witness trials, complete with judges in wigs and flowing robes. The courtrooms are open to the public Monday to Friday from 10am to 1pm and 2pm to 4pm. Be warned that cameras and bags aren't allowed in the building. The entrance to the public galleries is via Warwick Passage, about 1 block down Old Bailey on your left.

Leave the courthouse from the same doors that you entered through, and turn left onto Old Bailey. After 1 block, turn left onto Ludgate Hill. Cross Ave Maria Lane (named for the many religious processions held there in the Middle Ages), and continue half a block to:

27. **St. Paul's Cathedral** (© 020/7246 8357), where Prince Charles and the late Princess Diana wed. Dedicated to the patron saint of the City of London, St. Paul's is the masterpiece of architect Sir Christopher Wren. Wren is buried in the cathedral's crypt; his tomb bears the Latin inscription *lector, si monumentum requiris, circumspice* ("Reader, if you seek his monument, look around you"). To the left of the cathedral is:

28. **Temple Bar.** This gateway, designed by Sir Christopher Wren in the early 1670s, was used to mark the western boundary of the City of London. For over 200 years, London's masses passed through this magnificent creation, until the increased traffic of the Victorian metropolis rendered it little more than a " . . . leaden headed old obstruction . . ." to quote Charles Dickens. In 1877, it

was taken down and rebuilt in parkland 20 or so miles north of London, where it lay neglected and almost forgotten until the 2004 redevelopment of Pater Noster Square, the area of offices beyond. To mark the completion and opening of the project, Temple Bar was restored and re-erected alongside its architect's greatest achievement: St. Paul's Cathedral. See p. 34 in Walking Tour 2 for more about Temple Bar.

To reach St. Paul's Underground Station, exit the cathedral, continue along St. Paul's Churchyard, turn left at New Change, and continue until you reach Cheapside.

Dickens's London

Start: Holborn Underground Station.

Finish: Holborn Underground Station.

Time: 2½ hours.

Best Time: Monday to Friday from 1 to 4:30pm, when all the interiors on the tour are open.

Worst Time: Weekends (when much of the route is closed to the general public).

Charles Dickens was born in Portsmouth, England, on February 7, 1812. His family moved to London when he was 10, and within 2 years of the move, his life was thrown into turmoil when his father, John, was imprisoned for debt. Charles was sent to work at Warrens Blacking Warehouse, a boot-polish maker, entering the most miserable period of his childhood. Exactly how long he spent at Warrens is uncertain, but to the young Dickens it seemed like an eternity. This period was to have a profound influence on him both artistically and personally.

Dickens lived much of his life in London, and despite (or perhaps because of) his profound love/hate relationship with the city, his best works were written here. He loved to wander the streets for hours, day or night, and his novels often read like Victorian walking tours, packed with telling details. Everything he experienced registered in his photographic memory—from the sights and smells of his childhood to the faces and personalities of people he met in London's poorest quarters when he was an adult.

Although you won't find the deplorable conditions that prevailed in Dickens's time (overcrowded alleys, grimy buildings, coal pollution), you will discover unexpected spots of beauty, hidden passages, and courtyards that Dickens knew and loved.

• • • • • • • • • • • • • • • • •

Exit Holborn Underground Station, turn left onto Kingsway, and then make the third left into Remnant Street. One block ahead is:

1. **Lincoln's Inn Fields,** London's largest square. These fields were once farmland belonging to the duchess of Portsmouth. Dickens knew them well and featured them in his novel *Barnaby Rudge.*

   By keeping to the left side of Lincoln's Inn Fields, you'll arrive at:

2. **Sir John Soane's House,** 11 Lincoln's Inn Fields (✆ **020/7405-2107**), open Tuesday to Saturday from 10am to 5pm; admission is free. Sir John Soane, the architect of the Bank of England and 10 Downing St., lived in this house from 1792 until his death in 1837. The house was left to the nation and today calls itself a "museum." This, though, is a misleading term, for it's really Soane's personal collection of paintings and objects (from Greek vases to Egyptian scarabs), all still arranged as they were by Soane himself.

   Of particular interest from a "Dickensian" point of view are the originals of two series of paintings by William Hogarth: *The Rake's Progress* and *Election Campaign.* Hogarth was an astute observer of, and commentator on, the 18th-century social scene; his eye was every bit as keen as Dickens's for depicting London's low life, albeit in a

Dickens's London

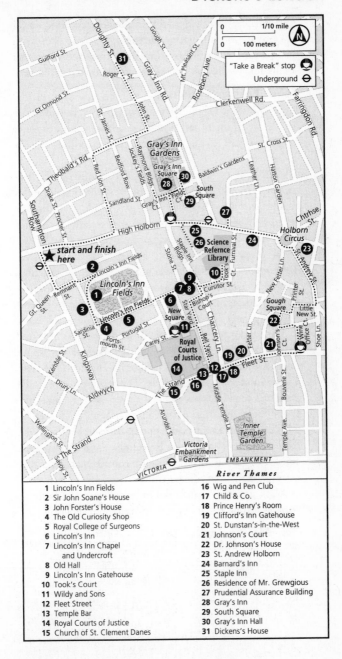

1 Lincoln's Inn Fields
2 Sir John Soane's House
3 John Forster's House
4 The Old Curiosity Shop
5 Royal College of Surgeons
6 Lincoln's Inn
7 Lincoln's Inn Chapel
   and Undercroft
8 Old Hall
9 Lincoln's Inn Gatehouse
10 Took's Court
11 Wildy and Sons
12 Fleet Street
13 Temple Bar
14 Royal Courts of Justice
15 Church of St. Clement Danes

16 Wig and Pen Club
17 Child & Co.
18 Prince Henry's Room
19 Clifford's Inn Gatehouse
20 St. Dunstan's-in-the-West
21 Johnson's Court
22 Dr. Johnson's House
23 St. Andrew Holborn
24 Barnard's Inn
25 Staple Inn
26 Residence of Mr. Grewgious
27 Prudential Assurance Building
28 Gray's Inn
29 South Square
30 Gray's Inn Hall
31 Dickens's House

different century and a different medium. He was a favorite artist of the young Dickens.

Exit right from the museum and retrace your footsteps counterclockwise around the square until you arrive at:

3. **John Forster's House,** 58 Lincoln's Inn Fields. Constructed in 1730, this house was divided in two in the 1790s, when the ornate porch was added. John Forster, a lawyer as well as the book and drama editor of *The Examiner,* lived here from 1834 to 1856. One of Dickens's best friends and a trusted confidant, he frequently accompanied Dickens on rambunctious rambles around the city. They often discussed work, and Dickens relied on Forster for business and creative advice. Forster went on to become Dickens's primary biographer.

In *Bleak House,* Dickens models the home of Mr. Tulkinghorn, a sinister lawyer, on this house. He describes it as "a large house, formerly a house of state . . . let off in chambers now; and in those shrunken fragments of greatness lawyers lie like maggots in nuts."

On December 2, 1844, in an upstairs room, Dickens gave a private reading from his sentimental Christmas novel *The Chimes.* The select gathering included the great Victorian sage Thomas Carlyle. The reading proved such a success that Dickens decided to repeat it 3 days later. From these informal gatherings, Dickens graduated to public readings that became so popular that he continued them all over Britain and later took them to America. These exhausting trips might have contributed to his premature death, at age 58, in 1870.

Walk straight out of Lincoln's Inn Fields onto Portsmouth Street. A few meters down on the left is:

4. **The Old Curiosity Shop,** 13–14 Portsmouth St. Predecessors of today's variety stores, curiosity shops sold such items as quill pens, paper, and other necessities and novelties. Constructed in 1567 from the wood of dismantled ships, this building first served as two laborers' cottages on farmland owned by the duchess of Portsmouth. It was remodeled as one building in the 18th century.

In Dickens's day, this store was owned by a bookbinder named Tessyman. It is believed that Tessyman's granddaughter inspired Dickens to create Little Nell, the child heroine of *The Old Curiosity Shop*. Although Dickens wrote that the actual shop that he "immortalized" was demolished in his lifetime, he would certainly have been familiar with this building, which currently houses a shop for custom-made shoes.

Return to Lincoln's Inn Fields and turn right, continuing counterclockwise around the square. The wonderful neoclassical building on your right is the:

5. **Royal College of Surgeons,** 35 Lincoln's Inn Fields. This impressive building from the 1830s was designed by Charles Barry, who also designed the Houses of Parliament. Dickens refers to it in *Bleak House,* when Mr. Boythorn comments that the lawyers of Lincoln's Inn should have their "necks rung and their skulls arranged in Surgeons Hall, for the contemplation of the whole profession, in order that its younger members might understand from actual measurement in early life, how thick skulls may become!"

The building is home to **The Museums of The Royal College of Surgeons of England** (*©* **020/7869-6560**). These include the **Hunterian Museum,** one of Britain's oldest and most important collections of human and zoological anatomy and pathology. Originally compiled by Dr. John Hunter (1728–93), see stop 2 in Walking Tour 9, p. 123, the displays of skulls—how many of which once belonged to lawyers is not recorded—brains, and other physiological delights, although fascinating, are certainly not for the squeamish. The museum is open to the public Monday to Friday from 10am to 5pm. Admission is free.

Exit Lincoln's Inn Fields through the ornate stone gate ahead and enter:

6. **Lincoln's Inn.** This compound is home to one of London's four Inns of Court, societies to which all aspiring and practicing barristers (lawyers) still belong. These institutions, dating back to the 14th century, were called "inns" because they provided room and board for their students. Today, tradition still requires legal apprentices to dine with their fraternity 24 times before they're admitted to the bar. Practicing barristers must continue to dine with the society at least three times during each law term in order to maintain their membership.

As you pass through the gates, look at the building immediately to your left. This is **Lincoln's Inn New Hall,** the barristers' dining hall, built in 1843. On the right is **New Square,** an office complex of barristers' chambers dating from the 1620s.

Walk under the brick archway directly ahead. To your left is:

7. **Lincoln's Inn Chapel and Undercroft.** This chapel was designed by Inigo Jones, one of London's most famous architects. In 1619, the building's foundation stone was laid by the renowned metaphysical poet/preacher John Donne, who also presided over the chapel's consecration on Ascension Day 1623. The undercroft (a covered, cloisterlike walkway) was intended to be a place where students could "walk and talk and confer for their learning," as well as a private spot where barristers could meet their clients. There are several tombstones along the undercroft, including that of John Thurloe, Secretary of State under Oliver Cromwell (Lord Protector, 1653–58).

The building to your right is the:

8. **Old Hall,** Lincoln's Inn, built in the second half of the 15th century. From 1737 to 1875, the hall housed the High Court of Chancery, England's court of finance and property, when the main court in Westminster Hall was on holiday. Dickens had worked as a court reporter at the Court of Chancery and disliked the place. The Old Hall and the Court of Chancery were targeted by Dickens's vitriolic pen in *Bleak House,* which told of the trial of *Jarndyce v. Jarndyce,* a case that had begun so long ago that no one could remember what it was about:

"This is the Court of Chancery; which has its decaying houses and its blighted lands in every shire; which has its worn-out lunatic in every madhouse, and its dead in every churchyard; which has its ruined suitor, with his slipshod heels and threadbare dress, borrowing and begging through the round of every man's acquaintance; which gives to monied might the means abundantly of wearying out the right; which so exhausts finances, patience, courage, hope; so overthrows the brain and breaks the heart; that there is not an honourable man among its practitioners who would not give—who does not often give—the warning, 'Suffer any wrong that can be done you, rather than come here!'"

Visitors aren't usually allowed into the Old Hall, but if the doors are open (which often happens), it can't hurt to try to look in.

Continue ahead, bear right across the courtyard, and exit Lincoln's Inn through:

9. **Lincoln's Inn Gatehouse,** built between 1517 and 1521 by Sir Thomas Lovell, the son of Henry VIII's chancellor. Above the outside doors you can see Lovell's coat of arms, together with those of Henry VIII and the Earl of Lincoln, this area's former landowner. According to biographer John Forster, when Dickens was a young boy, he was walking through this gate when "a big blackguard fellow walked up to me, doffed my cap and said 'hulloa soldier,' which I could not stand so I at once struck him and he then hit me in the eye."

Exit right through the gatehouse, cross over Chancery Lane, and make the first left into Cursitor Street. Continue for 1 block and turn left into:

10. **Took's Court.** In *Bleak House,* Dickens renamed this Cook's Court, and it's here that Mr. Snagsby, Law Stationer, "pursues his lawful calling . . . In the shade of Cook's Court, at most times a shady place, Mr. Snagsby had dealt in all sorts of blank forms of legal process." Today, this thin street still falls under the shade of tall buildings. Two 18th-century houses, one actually called Dickens House, lend it a dignified air.

Backtrack to Chancery Lane, turn left, and then take the first right (by the red mailbox) into Bishop's Court. Go left into Star Yard and turn right onto Carey Street. The first turn on your right brings you to Lincoln's Inn Archway, where you will find:

11. **Wildy and Sons,** Lincoln's Inn Archway, Carey Street (© 020/7242-5778), which has the distinction of being the oldest legal bookseller in London, having traded since 1798. You'll find new and secondhand law books, as well as collectible legal prints such as *The Law Suit,* a caricature of two farmers fighting over a cow—one pulls on the horns and the other pulls on the tail, while between them

sits the lawyer, milking the cow. The shop is open Monday to Friday from 8:45am to 5:15pm.

Return to Carey Street and continue along until you arrive at the:

☕ **Take a Break** **Seven Stars,** Carey Street (© 020/ 7242-8521). One of London's smallest pubs, this atmospheric place dates back to 1602 and is named for the seven provinces of the Netherlands. The pub is a favored haunt of lawyers and journalists enjoying a break from the rigors of the **Royal Courts of Justice** opposite, and chat is often about legal matters and gossip. Beers here include Directors and Courage Best, and good pub food is served.

Exit the pub and cross the street, turning left along Carey Street. Take the first turn right into Bell Yard and then make a right at the end onto:

12. **Fleet Street,** named for a nearby river (now covered over) that flows from Hampstead. This street is synonymous with journalism and once accommodated the printing facilities and offices of most London newspapers (as well as the barbershop of the bloodthirsty Sweeney Todd). The *Daily Telegraph* and *Daily Express* moved from their respective buildings several years ago, and no newspapers are headquartered here now. Dickens knew this area intimately and often walked along this street.

The monument in the center of the street is:

13. **Temple Bar.** This 6m-high (20 ft.) obelisk marks the boundary between the City of London (which you're about to leave) and Westminster. Its predecessor, a three-arched gateway (also called *Temple Bar*), was removed in 1877. It was to this predecessor that Dickens was referring in *Bleak House,* when he called it "that leaden-headed, old obstruction, appropriate ornament for the threshold of a leaden-headed old corporation: Temple Bar." In 2004, the original Temple Bar gateway was re-erected alongside St Paul's Cathedral (see stop 28 in Walking Tour 1, p. 25). As you pass the obelisk, notice that Fleet Street ends and the road changes its name to The Strand.

The buildings on your right are the:

14. **Royal Courts of Justice,** designed and built by architect George Street between 1872 and 1882. This spectacular Gothic building was erected with about 35 million bricks and boasts more than 1,000 rooms and more than 5.6km (3½ miles) of corridors. Stand directly outside the main entrance and look up to see a sculpture of Christ, flanked by statues of King Solomon (left) and King Alfred (right).

    Inside the main hall of this high English court is a small exhibit of the official garments worn by judges and barristers. You're free to walk around the building and glance into the courtrooms. Here, and in the halls, you may see judges dressed in ermine-trimmed robes and full-bottomed wigs. Cameras aren't allowed inside.

    Cross over the pedestrian crossing outside the Royal Courts. To your right is the:

15. **Church of St. Clement Danes.** Inside is a memorial to members of the U.S. Air Force who were stationed in England during World War II.

    Turn left on the opposite side and backtrack along The Strand. Just past the next crossing, you'll come to the:

16. **Wig and Pen Club,** 229–230 The Strand. Begun in 1625, this famous fraternity survived the Great Fire of London (1666) and was once the city's most exclusive club for lawyers and journalists. At the time of writing, the building had been closed for over a year, and its future appears uncertain.

    Continue walking along The Strand and back into Fleet Street; just beyond Temple Bar on the right is:

17. **Child & Co.,** 1 Fleet St., a private bank started by Francis Child in 1673. Child's bank was the model for Tellson's Bank in Dickens's *A Tale of Two Cities.* In the glass case opposite the door, you can see the guns purchased by the bank governors to protect their establishment from the threat posed by the Gordon riots of 1780. Led by Lord George Gordon, this anti-Catholic uprising was the subject of Dickens's novel *Barnaby Rudge.*

    Continue along Fleet Street. To the right of the traffic lights is:

18. **Prince Henry's Room,** 17 Fleet St. (no phone), contained in a fantastically preserved building from 1610. It is believed that this room was the office of Prince Henry, who was the Duke of Cornwall and Prince of Wales. The building that houses the room is one of the few remaining wooden structures that survived London's Great Fire of 1666.

Originally an inn called the Princes Arms, the building later housed Mrs. Salmon's Waxworks, a kind of early Madame Tussaud's that became a favorite haunt of the young Dickens. In *David Copperfield,* Dickens's hero goes "to see some perspiring wax works in Fleet Street." Today Prince Henry's Room is a museum focusing on 17th-century diarist Samuel Pepys (see stop 3 in Walking Tour 3, p. 46), and it is open Monday to Saturday from 11am to 2pm. Admission is free.

The staircase to the left of the front gates takes you up to the small, beautifully constructed room. A set of three feathers appears on the ceiling (the symbol of the Prince of Wales), together with Prince Henry's initials. Henry was the eldest son of James I; his untimely death at the age of 18 enabled his brother, Charles I, to inherit the throne.

Cross Fleet Street via the pedestrian crossing, turn right, and, just past Chancery Lane, turn left into the narrow alleyway called Clifford's Inn Passage. At the end of the alley is the 17th-century:

19. **Clifford's Inn Gatehouse,** all that remains of the Old Inn. This was a prep school for aspiring attorneys from the 15th through the 18th centuries. In Dickens's *Little Dorrit,* Little Dorrit's brother, Tip, finds "a stool and twelve shillings a week in the office of the attorney in Clifford's Inn and here languished for six months."

This was a rather unpleasant place in Dickens's day. In *Our Mutual Friend,* John Rokesmith, a principal character, meets Mr. Boffin on the street and says: "'Would you object to turn aside into this place—I think it is called Clifford's Inn—where we can hear one another better than in the roaring street?' Mr. Boffin glanced into the mouldy little plantation, or cat-preserve, of Clifford's Inn as it was that day . . . Sparrows were there, dry rot and wet rot were there but it was not otherwise a suggestive spot."

Return to Fleet Street and turn left; two doors along is:

20. **St. Dunstan's-in-the-West,** Fleet Street, an octagonal church. The large clock on the tower was installed by the congregation to express its thanks that the building was spared from the Great Fire. However, the original church was entirely replaced between 1829 and 1833. The present building is an excellent early example of Gothic Revival architecture. The clock dates to 1671; its two giant clubs still strike a reverberating bell every 15 minutes. This was the first clock in London with a double face and with minutes marked on its dial. Dickens mentions the clock in both *Barnaby Rudge* and *David Copperfield.*

    Opposite the interior door is a beautiful **icon screen** brought here from Antim Monastery in Bucharest.

    Exit the church, turn left, and continue along Fleet Street. Two doors away (just after no. 185), turn into **Hen and Chickens Court,** an extremely Dickensian inner court. It was here, in the Victorian melodrama, that the fictitious shop of Sweeney Todd, the Demon Barber of Fleet Street, was located. Return to Fleet Street and cross Fetter Lane. Just past the bus stop, on your left, is:

21. **Johnson's Court.** Although nothing from Dickens's day survives on this street, the writer's career began here. This was once the address of *Monthly Magazine*'s office. John Forster wrote that Dickens, "stealthily one evening at twilight," dropped off, "with fear and trembling," an article that *Monthly Magazine* accepted. It became his first published piece. This, as well as other early works by Dickens, was published under the pseudonym "Boz," his younger brother's nickname.

    Continue 2 blocks farther along Fleet Street and turn left into Wine Office Court. A few meters up on the right is:

☕ **Take a Break** Ye Olde Cheshire Cheese, Wine Office Court, 145 Fleet St. (℡ **020/7353-6170**). This is one of the city's oldest pubs and was one of Dickens's favorite watering holes. There has been a tavern here since the 1590s, and the vaulted cellar might have been part of the Old Whitefriars Monastery that once occupied this site. After it burned down in the Great Fire, Ye Olde Cheshire

Cheese was quickly rebuilt, becoming the first pub to reopen after the fire. Downstairs, you can still see charred wooden beams that date back to the fire.

Dickens's regular table, mentioned in *A Tale of Two Cities,* was to the right of the fireplace, in the room directly on the left as you enter.

Earlier in the twentieth century, the pub gained an additional measure of fame thanks to its foul-mouthed mascot, Polly the parrot. On Armistice Day, 1918, the bird imitated the popping of a champagne cork 400 times and then fainted; throughout the 1920s, Polly was renowned for her ability to swear in several languages. Her 1926 death was announced on the BBC World Service, and the *London Times* carried her obituary under the headline "International Expert in Profanity Dies." You can find Polly, now stuffed and mounted and looking somewhat bedraggled, in the "Chop Room" located immediately on the left as you enter.

Continue through Wine Office Court, bear left at the tree, and walk half a block into Gough *(Goff)* Square to:

22. **Dr. Johnson's House,** 17 Gough Sq. (© 020/7353-3745). A significant literary scholar and critic, Samuel Johnson (1709–1784) lived and worked here, compiling the world's first English-language dictionary. Johnson lived quite humbly: When artist Joshua Reynolds visited Dr. Johnson's long attic, he observed that "besides his books, all covered with dust, there was an old crazy meal table, and still worse, an older elbow chair having only three legs." Johnson's house is now a museum of memorabilia, featuring portraits of his circle of friends as well as his original dictionary. The museum is open Monday to Saturday from 11am to 5pm. Admission is charged.

Exit Gough Square through the passage opposite Dr. Johnson's House. Turn left onto Gunpowder Square, and then head straight to Printer Street. Turn right onto Little New Street and left onto Shoe Lane, which after 2 blocks becomes St. Andrew Street. Continue 230m (754 ft.) ahead to Holborn Circus. The **statue** in the center of the road is of Queen Victoria's consort, Prince Albert. He's raising his hat to the City of London, an act that has led this work to be dubbed "London's politest statue." On the corner to your right is:

23. **St. Andrew Holborn,** Holborn Circus, the largest Sir Christopher Wren–designed parish church. Upon his death in 1348, a local merchant, John Thane, willed all his houses and shops to this church; his bequest provides for the church's upkeep to this day. There has been a succession of churches on this site since the year 951. The present building, which was damaged by air raids during World War II, was restored in 1961. Dickens mentions St. Andrew in *Oliver Twist:* The burglar Bill Sykes looks up at the clock tower and says to Oliver, "Hard upon seven! You must step out." The two leave from here and rob a house.

Turn left onto Holborn and walk 1 block. Just after the HSBC bank, you'll see the entrance to:

24. **Barnard's Inn,** a former prep school for students of the Inns of Court. It can be confusing that so many buildings are called "inns," and apparently Dickens thought so too. In *Great Expectations,* the protagonist, Pip, says of Barnard's, "I had supposed that establishment to be a hotel kept by Mr. Barnard. Whereas I now found Barnard to be a disembodied spirit, or a fiction, and his inn the dingiest collection of shabby buildings ever squeezed together in a rank corner as a club for Tom-cats."

One block ahead on Holborn, on the left, is:

25. **Staple Inn,** headquarters of the Institute of Actuaries. The inn, whose timber front dates from 1576, is London's last existing example of domestic architecture from Shakespeare's day. It was originally a hostel for wool staplers, or brokers, thus the name. Walk through the gates, where a sign on your left warns: "The porter has orders to prevent old clothes men and others from calling 'articles for sale'"—in other words, "No soliciting."

Once inside, you'll find yourself in a rare tranquil oasis that Dickens appreciated. As he wrote in *The Mystery of Edwin Drood:* "Behind the most ancient part of Holborn, London, where certain gabled houses some centuries of age still stand looking on the public way . . . is a little nook called Staple Inn. It is one of those nooks the turning into which out of the clashing streets, imparts to the relieved pedestrian the sensation of having put cotton in his ears and velvet soles on his boots." Pause and consider just how little this place has changed since Dickens wrote those sentences.

Cross the cobblestone courtyard, walk through the covered passageway, and look at the building immediately on your left. This was the:

26. **Residence of Mr. Grewgious,** the kindly lawyer in *The Mystery of Edwin Drood.* A stone above the door bears the inscription "PJT 1747." In the novel, Dickens wondered why Grewgious wasn't curious about what PJT might stand for, other than "perhaps John Thomas" or "probably Joe Tyler." In fact, the initials are those of the inn's then-president, John Thompson.

Follow the unmarked walkway as it bears right, climb the steps, and turn right onto the pedestrian walkway called Staple Inn Buildings. At the end, find the entrance to Chancery Lane Underground Station. Use this underpass to cross under Holborn; once past the telephones, take the exit on your right through the tunnel. Go up the stairs and walk half a block to London's last great example of Gothic Revival architecture, the:

27. **Prudential Assurance Building.** This large structure of red brick and terra cotta was designed by Alfred Waterhouse in 1879. Enter through the gates opposite the bus stop and cross to the other side; in a small grotto you'll see a bust of Dickens. The Prudential Building stands on the site of Furnivals Inn, where Dickens lived from 1834 to 1837. It was during this time that Dickens began writing *The Pickwick Papers,* the work that secured his literary fame.

Return to Holborn and turn right. Cross Gray's Inn Road and continue along Holborn until you reach the:

Take a Break **Citte of York Pub,** 22–23 High Holborn (☎ **020/7242-7670**). Even though it's one of the largest pubs around, this grand Victorian-style tavern offers unparalleled intimacy in cozy cubicles. Once popular with lawyers seeking a place to speak confidentially with clients, the pub now draws many office workers. In the cellar is a second bar.

Exit the pub and immediately turn left down a small alley to:

28. **Gray's Inn,** another of London's four Inns of Court and one that certainly didn't impress Dickens. In *The Uncommercial Traveller,* he wrote: "Indeed, I look upon Gray's Inn generally as one of the most depressing institutions in brick and mortar known to the children of men."

The passageway opens up into a part of the inn called:

29. **South Square.** In 1828, when Dickens was 16, he worked here as a clerk for the law firm Ellis and Blackmore (1 South Sq.). The mischievous author-to-be used to drop small stones from the upstairs windows onto the heads of unsuspecting lawyers. Dickens learned shorthand here because his father felt that the training would enable him to become a reporter at Doctors Commons (the College of Advocates and Doctors of Law). Although Dickens's career goals changed, the shorthand he learned probably led to his phonetic style of writing. If you look inside the front entrance of **1 South Square,** you'll see a portrait of Dickens as a young man.

The black **statue** on the far side of the lawn is of Sir Francis Bacon, Lord Chancellor of England under Elizabeth I, and a writer, philosopher, and influential scientific theorist. Bacon's best-known work is his *Essays,* remarkable for their pithy, epigrammatic style. The statue was erected in 1912 and shows Bacon wearing his official robes.

The churchlike building at the far side of the square is:

30. **Gray's Inn Hall.** Built in 1556, this hall hosted the first performance of Shakespeare's *Comedy of Errors* in 1594. Both the hall and South Square are mentioned in many of Dickens's novels. From *The Pickwick Papers:* "Clerk after clerk hastened into the square by one or other of the entrances, and looking up at the hall clock accelerated or decreased his rate of walking according to the time at which his office hours nominally commenced."

Exit South Square on the road running along the left side of Gray's Inn Hall and take the first left onto the path running under the buildings. Pass the gardens and take the first right onto Gray's Inn Place (the sign reads TO RAYMOND BUILDINGS). Continue ahead through the main gates and turn right onto Theobald's Road. Take the first left onto John Street, which becomes Doughty Street. About 5 blocks ahead, on your right, is:

31. **Dickens's House,** 48 Doughty St. (© 020/7405-2127), the author's only surviving London home. Dickens moved into this modest dwelling in 1837, before he was well known. While living here, he finished *The Pickwick Papers* as well as *Oliver Twist* and *Nicholas Nickleby,* and he started work on *Barnaby Rudge.* By the time he left this house in 1839, Dickens was a world-renowned writer. You can see the author's letters, furniture, and first editions in glass display cases, adjacent to rooms that have been restored. The house is open Monday to Saturday from 10am to 5pm; there's an admission charge.

Return to Theobald's Road and turn right. Four blocks along, turn left into Red Lion Street; at the end, turn right onto High Holborn. Keep to the left side to arrive back at Holborn Underground Station.

A Historic Pub Walk

Start: Embankment Underground Station.

Finish: Covent Garden Underground Station.

Time: 2½ hours, including pauses to quench your thirst.

Best Time: During pub hours, Monday to Saturday from 11am to 11pm, or Sunday from noon to 10:30pm. If you take your walk around lunchtime, you can sample traditional "pub grub." After 5pm or around sunset is a good time to drink with the locals.

Worst Time: Late at night, when the streets are dark, or Sundays, when many sights are closed.

There's nothing more British than a pub. In fact, pubs are almost as old as England itself. In the 12th century, William Fitzstephen (secretary to Thomas à Becket) noted that London was cursed by two plagues: fire and drink. The public house is exactly that—the British public's place to meet, exchange stories, tell jokes, grab a quick bite, and drink. Many efforts have been made to create something resembling a pub outside Britain, but they just don't capture the unique feel of the real McCoy. An occasional afternoon—or, more often, evening—spent in a pub is part of British social life. And on Sunday afternoons, entire families often go to the pub for lunch. (Note, however, that children under 14 aren't allowed into pubs that don't serve food, and no one under 18 may legally be served alcohol. Children under 14 can sit outside in summer, though few pubs in central London have outside seating.)

Beer is the principal drink sold in pubs, available in Imperial half-pints and pints (20% larger than U.S. measures). The choice is usually between lager and bitter. Lagers are what Americans and Australians tend to think of as "beer," while bitters are more . . . well . . . bitter. Locals usually prefer the latter. Many pubs serve particularly good "real" ales, which can be distinguished at the bar by hand pumps that the barkeeps must "pull." Real ales are natural "live" beers that have been allowed to ferment in the cask. Unlike lagers, English ales are served at room temperature and might take some getting used to for the novice. For an unusual and tasty alternative, try cider, a flavorful fermented apple juice that's so good you'll hardly notice the alcohol—until later.

As a rule, there's no table service in pubs; you order drinks and food at the bar and carry everything to your table. Tipping isn't customary and should be reserved for exemplary service. Pubs are generally open 11am to 11pm Monday to Saturday and noon to 10:30pm on Sunday. At press time, the drinks industry was undergoing one of its biggest shake-ups in history: pubs are about to choose their own hours, and round-the-clock drinking will become a possibility in London. Most publicans will probably apply for extended hours on Thursdays, Fridays, and Saturdays, sticking to the time-honored traditional opening hours for the rest of the week.

Carpeted floors, etched glass, and carved-wood bars are the hallmarks of most pubs. But each one looks different, and each has its own individual atmosphere and clientele. Greater London's 7,000-plus pubs mean that you'll never have to walk more than a few blocks to find one, and part of the enjoyment of "pubbing" is discovering a hidden special spot all on your own. This tour will take you to some of the most famous, as well as some of the least known, watering holes in the city—an excellent cross-section of taverns united by their ties to London's past. Cheers!

A Historic Pub Walk

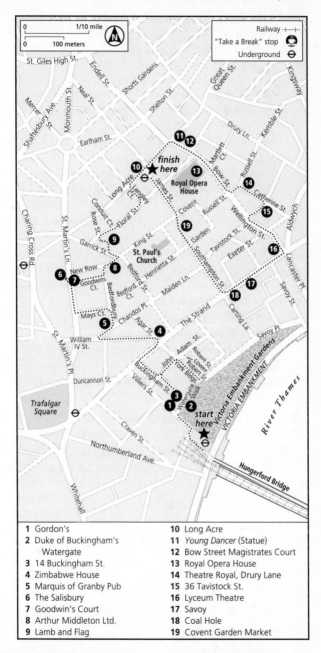

1 Gordon's
2 Duke of Buckingham's
   Watergate
3 14 Buckingham St.
4 Zimbabwe House
5 Marquis of Granby Pub
6 The Salisbury
7 Goodwin's Court
8 Arthur Middleton Ltd.
9 Lamb and Flag
10 Long Acre
11 *Young Dancer* (Statue)
12 Bow Street Magistrates Court
13 Royal Opera House
14 Theatre Royal, Drury Lane
15 36 Tavistock St.
16 Lyceum Theatre
17 Savoy
18 Coal Hole
19 Covent Garden Market

Take the left exit from Embankment Underground Station and walk up Villiers Street. Don't walk too far, though. The first brown wooden door on your right is the entrance to:

1. **Gordon's,** 47 Villiers St. Gordon's may be the most atmospheric and eccentric wine bar you'll ever visit. Though it's not a pub, Gordon's unusual decor and atmosphere make it a great first stop on this tour. The candlelit drinking room features intimate, low-vaulted ceilings. Framed yellowed newspapers adorn the walls; model Spitfires, covered in dust, hang from the ceiling; and rickety tables crowd the floor. Famous past customers have included G. K. Chesterton and Rudyard Kipling, among others.

    Like other wine bars in London, Gordon's is an excellent alternative to the traditional pub, offering a good selection of vino by the glass or bottle, plus food that meets relatively high standards

    Note that, unusually, this bar is not open at all on either Saturday or Sunday.

    Leaving Gordon's, turn left onto Villiers Street and immediately left again down the steps to Watergate Walk. Stroll along the pathway until, half a block ahead on your right, you come to the:

2. **Duke of Buckingham's Watergate.** Before the late-19th-century construction of the Victoria Embankment, this stone gateway marked the river's high-tide line and protected the duke's mansion (which once stood behind it). The inscription on top of the gate reads FIDEI COTICULA CRUX ("The cross is the touchstone of faith")—the duke's family motto. After the mansion was demolished in 1675, the grounds were turned into a public park. These are the gardens where George Orwell slept while living as a vagrant in the 1930s; he later wrote about this experience in *Down and Out in Paris and London.*

    With your back to the watergate, climb the flight of stone steps, walk through the iron gate, and enter Buckingham Street. On your left is:

3. **14 Buckingham St.,** the former home of Samuel Pepys (1633–1703). Despite a long and distinguished career as

an official in naval affairs, Pepys is best remembered for the detailed diary he kept from 1660 to 1669. Pepys's diary is not only an important record of the events and manners of his day but also a fascinating psychological study of the diarist himself. Thanks to his writings, we know more about Pepys than about any other person of his time. Most of Pepys's entries were written at night by candlelight, a practice that eventually ruined his eyesight. Pepys concealed the contents of the diary from his wife by using his own personal code—a complex mix of foreign and invented words. It was probably a smart move to use this code: Upon returning home after an evening spent with an actress, he wrote that his wife pulled aside the bed curtain and with red-hot tongs "made as if she did design to pinch me with them." The diarist moved from this house in 1701, 2 years before his death.

This area (encompassing the site of Pepys's house) was developed in the late 18th century as a housing project called **Adelphi.** It was initiated by three brothers—John, Robert, and James Adam (*Adelphoi* is Greek for broth-ers)—and financed by a lottery with the approval of an act of Parliament. The houses were built on arches, vaults, and subterranean streets so that they'd rise above the mud of the Thames. Few of these arches now remain, but if you turn right on John Adam Street, right again on York Buildings, and then left into the narrow Lower Robert Street, you can explore one of these vaults. Within their confines, in years past, "the most abandoned characters have often passed the night, nestling upon foul straw; and many a street thief escaped from his pursuers in these dis-mal haunts."

Return to John Adam Street and look to the right toward the attractive dark house with the ornate cream columns and windows. This is **7 Adam Street,** and it origi-nally belonged to Robert Adam, one of the founding brothers of the Adelphi housing project.

Return to the junction of York Buildings and John Adam Street. From York Buildings, cross John Adam Street and go straight ahead into George Court. Climb the steps onto The Strand, cross at the crosswalk, turn right at the corner of Agar Street, and pause by:

4. **Zimbabwe House,** the home of the Zimbabwe High Commission. Look up at the second-story windows, between which stand nude statues depicting the Ages of Man. The figures caused such an outcry when they were unveiled by sculptor Jacob Epstein in 1908 that the windows of the building across the street were replaced with frosted glass to obscure the view. After the Southern Rhodesian High Commission moved into the building in the 1930s, one of the statues' "private" parts broke off and nearly struck a pedestrian below. Orders were given to "remove the protruding parts" of the statues, and they remain castrated to this day.

Turn sharply left onto William IV Street, and then take the first right into Chandos Place. On the next corner is the:

5. **Marquis of Granby Pub,** 51 Chandos Place. This tavern dates from the reign of Charles II (1660–1685), when it was known as the "Hole in the Wall" and was run by an ex-mistress of the second duke of Buckingham. The pub was renamed in the late 18th century in honor of Gen. John Manners, the marquis of Granby. Manners led the English army in 1759 at the Battle of Minden, one of the battles that helped the English secure a victory over France in the Seven Years' War. In the 19th century, Claude Duval, one of England's most notorious robbers and a consummate ladies' man, was arrested while drinking here. After his trial and execution, Duval was buried beneath a tombstone that reads:

> *Here lies Duval.*
> *Reader: if male thou art, look to thy purse*
> *If female, to thy heart.*

Today, the cheerful English-inn atmosphere makes this place popular with actors and workers from the nearby theaters. The pub serves several cask-conditioned "real" ales, a monthly guest beer, and a traditional menu (until 5pm). It's especially busy at lunchtime.

Exit the pub and turn left onto Bedfordbury. Go past the stage doors of London Coliseum (home of the English National Opera) and turn left onto Mays Court. Turn right onto St. Martin's Lane, cross over, and keep to its left side to arrive at:

6. **The Salisbury,** 90 St. Martin's Lane. Formerly known as the Coach and Horses, and later as Ben Caunts' Head, this 1852 tavern gained fame for the bare-knuckle prize-fights that used to take place here. The magnificent marble fittings, cut-glass mirrors, brass statuettes, plush seats, and Art Nouveau decor—all beautifully preserved—make this one of the most attractive pubs in London. A quintessential theater pub, the Salisbury touts itself as the "archetype of actors' pubs, and as much a part of the world of the stage as greasepaint."

   Leave the Salisbury and bear right across St. Martin's Lane. Almost directly ahead, climb the two steps at 55–56 St. Martin's Lane to enter:

7. **Goodwin's Court,** a little-known, wonderfully preserved 18th-century street. At night, the bucolic gas lamp–lit court feels like a Hollywood set. It's magical.

   Walk through Goodwin's Court and turn left on Bedfordbury. On the corner of New Row is:

8. **Arthur Middleton Ltd.,** 12 New Row, purveyors of antique scientific tools and instruments. Take a look inside; you might find centuries-old telescopes, weather-data devices, and surgical instruments. The window displays are usually rather interesting as well.

   Turn right onto New Row, left onto Garrick Street, and then immediately right onto Rose Street to the:

9. **Lamb and Flag,** 33 Rose St. Built in 1623, this wood-frame structure is remarkable in that it survived not only the Great Fire of 1666, but all of the city's other blazes. A favorite haunt of Charles Dickens, this pub was once known as the "Bucket of Blood" because of the prizefights held here for betting customers. Poet John Dryden (1631–1700) was attacked and beaten in the side alley by thugs, probably hired by the Earl of Rochester, who was unhappy about a vicious lampoon that Dryden had written about him.

   Leave the pub by the side exit, turn left down the narrow wood-lined alley called Lazenby Court, and turn right onto upscale Floral Street. After about 275m (902 ft.), turn left onto Langley Court and then right onto:

10. **Long Acre,** Covent Garden's main thoroughfare and a popular shopping street. Long Acre connects Covent Garden with Leicester Square. At night, especially on weekends, this is one of the busiest streets in London.

    Walk about 3 blocks (along which you'll find great window-shopping) past the Covent Garden Underground Station; turn right onto Bow Street, and take the first left to see:

11. **Young Dancer,** a beautiful statue by Enzo Plazzotta (1921–81), on your left. London is packed with outdoor statues—some 1,700 at last count—but most are old memorials to even older statesmen. *Young Dancer* is one of London's few examples of good modern outdoor sculpture. This statue honors the dancers of the Royal Ballet, who perform at the Royal Opera House (just across the street).

    Next to the statue, on the corner, is the:

12. **Bow Street Magistrates Court.** Henry Fielding, author of *The History of Tom Jones,* became a Justice of the Peace in 1747 and ran his court at 4 Bow St. (now demolished). Along with his blind half brother, John, Fielding helped establish the Bow Street Runners, London's first salaried, permanent police force. At the time of writing, discussions are taking place over plans to turn this building into a hotel.

    Opposite the court is the:

13. **Royal Opera House** (℡ 020/7304-4000), home to both the Royal Opera and the Royal Ballet. Originally called the Theatre Royal Covent Garden, this is the third theater to stand on this site (the previous two were destroyed by fire). On either side of the portico are stone carvings from the preceding theater—*The Comic Muse,* by John Flaxman, and *The Tragic Muse,* by J. C. Rossi. These sculptors also created the frieze across the front of the building. The present theater, designed by E. M. Barry, opened in 1858.

    In 1919, Lowell Thomas introduced the British public to Lawrence of Arabia at this theater. The audience gave the film a standing ovation, and the *Times* critic wrote that it was "a triumphant vindication of the power of moving pictures, accompanied by a spoken story, to charm the eye, entertain the spirit, and move to its very depths the soul." Soon, audiences were lining up all night in hopes of getting in to see the film. The only person who complained was T. E. Lawrence himself; he said that his life had become very difficult since eager crowds began surrounding him on the street. However, Lawrence and Thomas became good friends. Thomas was often asked for anecdotes about Lawrence, and when Thomas tried to check out one story, Lawrence laughed and said: "Use it if it suits your needs. What difference does it make if it's true? History is seldom true."

The opera house recently underwent massive renovations; it now boasts some of the most advanced computerized set-changing technology in the world. You can explore this equipment on backstage tours, offered Monday to Saturday at 10:30am, 12:30pm, and 2:30pm. There is a charge.

Continue 2 blocks down Bow Street, turn left onto Russell Street, and then immediately turn right onto Catherine Street to the:

14. **Theatre Royal, Drury Lane,** Catherine Street (© **020/7850-8791**), one of London's oldest theaters. This theater was opened under a royal charter in 1663 by playwright/Poet Laureate Thomas Killigrew (believed to be the illegitimate son of Shakespeare). Killigrew also made theatrical history by hiring, in 1666, the first female actor to perform professionally on the English stage.

In 1742, David Garrick, one of the city's most famous actors, made his debut here. Five years later, he became the theater's manager and staged numerous Shakespearean revivals. The theater changed hands in 1777, when it was taken over by Richard Brinsley Sheridan. Unfortunately, the building wasn't insured, and when it caught fire in 1809, all Sheridan could do was sit with a glass of port and watch the blaze, commenting that "surely a man may take a glass of wine by his own fireside." The present building, from 1812, is modeled after the Grand Théâtre at Bordeaux. Major musicals are often staged here.

Jerome Kern's *Showboat* opened at the theater in 1929, with Paul Robeson singing the lead role. Robeson's rendition of "Ol' Man River" made him an overnight celebrity. Afterward, he remarked that England seemed to be relatively free of racial prejudice. As it happened, however, a celebration was held in his honor at the Savoy Grill Room—and he was refused entrance. This embarrassing and egregious mistake even reached discussion in the House of Commons.

Guided tours of the theater are available on Monday, Tuesday, Thursday, Friday, and Sunday at 2:15 and 4:45pm; and Wednesday and Saturday at 10:15am and noon. There is a charge. For reservations, call ℭ **020/ 7850-8791.**

Continue down Catherine Street and turn right on Tavistock Street. Across the road is:

15. **36 Tavistock St.,** the former home of Thomas de Quincey (1785–1859), author of *Confessions of an English Opium Eater.* When de Quincey was a young man, he started taking opium to numb the effects of a painful gastric disease. Before long, he became heavily addicted and, for most of his life, was just barely able to support his family by writing newspaper and magazine articles. As an old man, he became a celebrated eccentric—alone and poverty stricken.

Just a few steps ahead, turn left onto Wellington Street. Walk down the hill until, on the right, you come to the:

16. **Lyceum Theatre,** built in 1771. Over the years this building has housed theatrical performances, a circus, and (in 1802) Madame Tussaud's first London Waxworks exhibitions. Its heyday was perhaps the late 19th century, when Henry Irving and Ellen Terry performed here in a number of Shakespearean plays. In the 1960s, when the building was a dance hall, John Lennon staged the first public performance of his Plastic Ono Band. The theater is still in operation, under the ownership of Andrew Lloyd Webber.

Turn right on The Strand. At the traffic lights, immediately cross over to the south side of the street. Continue 1 block and turn left into the forecourt of the:

17. **Savoy.** This hotel was built in 1889 by impresario Richard D'Oyly Carte as an adjunct to his theater. In

August 1914, the hotel became something of a focal point for the estimated 150,000 American tourists who found themselves stranded in Europe at the outbreak of World War I. Because numerous banks had closed, many tourists discovered that they were without money and without the means to book a hotel room or a cabin on a steamer. At the Savoy, they formed a committee, later headed by Herbert Hoover, to contact American firms in London requesting a loan of money. Over the course of 6 weeks, these firms loaned $150 million, enabling most of the travelers to return home. (One woman asked the committee for a written guarantee that the ship she'd be sailing on wouldn't be torpedoed by the Germans; it obliged.) It's interesting to note that nearly everyone made good on his or her loan repayment—only about $300 was never repaid.

Continuing a little way along The Strand will bring you to the:

18. **Coal Hole,** 91 The Strand. This is one of central London's largest pubs, established in the early 19th century for the coal haulers who unloaded boats on the Thames. Like many other pubs in and around the West End, the Coal Hole has numerous theatrical connections. In the mid–19th century, actor Edmund Kean hired gangs of rowdies and got them drunk here before sending them to Drury Lane's rival theaters to heckle the actors and cause trouble. Look for an inscription on one of the pub's interior wooden beams commemorating the Wolf Club, an informal group organized by Kean for men whose wives didn't allow them to sing in the bath.

Cross The Strand and continue straight ahead to Southampton Street. Walk up the hill to:

19. **Covent Garden Market**, whose name derives from the convent garden of Westminster Abbey, which once occupied this space. Designed in the 1630s by Inigo Jones, one of London's most famous architects, this was a residential square that eventually fell into disrepair. All that remains of Jones's architecture is **St. Paul's Church,** on the west side of the square. The opening scene of George Bernard Shaw's *Pygmalion* (1913) takes place outside St. Paul's,

where Professor Henry Higgins meets the flower seller Eliza Doolittle.

A flower and vegetable market occupied this spot from 1860 to 1974. Today, you'll find a covered mall packed with interesting shops, restaurants, sidewalk cafes, pubs, street performers, and tourists.

The three pubs on the north side of the market (toward Covent Garden Underground Station) are all top picks for cozy comfort and lively atmosphere (as well as above-average pub grub). Any one of them would make a fine place to end your historic walk.

Cross to the opposite side of the market and walk up James Street to arrive at Covent Garden Underground Station.

Westminster & Whitehall

Start: Trafalgar Square.

Finish: Westminster Underground Station.

Time: 1½ hours, not including museum stops.

Best Time: When the museums are open, Monday to Saturday from 10am to 5:30pm, and Sunday from 2 to 5:30pm.

Worst Time: Early Sunday, when the museums are closed.

Whitehall, the important thoroughfare that leads off Trafalgar Square, is the center of government. Much of the street was fronted by the old Palace of Whitehall until it burned down in 1698. Today, many government departments have a Whitehall address. The official residence of the prime minister is just steps away, on Downing Street, and a short distance away, the spectacular Houses of Parliament tower over Parliament Square.

This walk parallels the Thames and takes you past some of London's most famous buildings and monuments of historic and contemporary interest.

Start at Trafalgar Square, which you can reach by taking the Tube to the Charing Cross or Embankment Underground Stations (within 1 block of each other). Be careful of traffic as you cross to the center of:

1. **Trafalgar Square,** the heart of London. To the east is the City, London's financial center. To the north are Leicester Square and the commercial West End, London's entertainment and shopping areas. To the west is The Mall, the royal road that leads to Buckingham Palace. And to the south is Whitehall, the nation's street of government. The entire square is the site of London's large annual New Year's Eve party. At the center of pigeon-infested Trafalgar Square is:

2. **Nelson's Column,** one of the most famous monuments in London, commemorating Viscount Horatio Nelson's victory over a French and Spanish fleet at the Battle of Trafalgar in 1805. The column is topped with a granite statue of Lord Nelson standing 5m (17 ft.) high. It's so heavy that it had to be hoisted up in three sections.

   At the base of the column are the famous **Bronze Lions** and **Trafalgar Fountains.** Of the three other sculptures in Trafalgar Square, the most interesting is the:

3. **Equestrian statue of George IV,** which was intended to top the Marble Arch which now stands at the northeast corner of Hyde Park. George was known to his contemporaries as the First Gentleman of Europe, which led one poet to compose the following lampoon:

   A noble, nasty course he ran
   Superbly filthy and fastidious,
   He was the world's first gentleman
   And made that appellation hideous.

   Leave the square on the north side and walk over to the:

4. **National Gallery** (© 020/7839-3321), a cupola-topped building that houses Britain's finest collection of paintings by world-class masters including Rembrandt, Raphael, Botticelli, Goya, and Hogarth. The permanent collection, arranged by school, includes representative works from almost every major European artist from the

Westminster & Whitehall

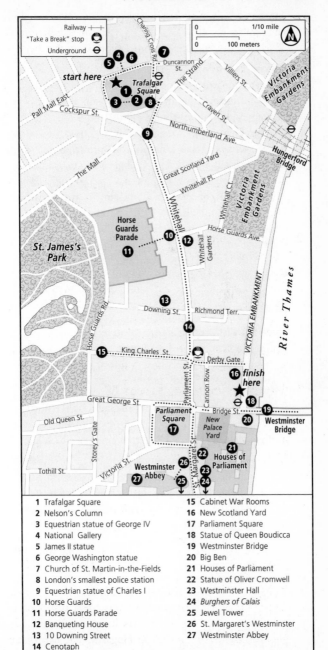

1 Trafalgar Square
2 Nelson's Column
3 Equestrian statue of George IV
4 National Gallery
5 James II statue
6 George Washington statue
7 Church of St. Martin-in-the-Fields
8 London's smallest police station
9 Equestrian statue of Charles I
10 Horse Guards
11 Horse Guards Parade
12 Banqueting House
13 10 Downing Street
14 Cenotaph
15 Cabinet War Rooms
16 New Scotland Yard
17 Parliament Square
18 Statue of Queen Boudicca
19 Westminster Bridge
20 Big Ben
21 Houses of Parliament
22 Statue of Oliver Cromwell
23 Westminster Hall
24 *Burghers of Calais*
25 Jewel Tower
26 St. Margaret's Westminster
27 Westminster Abbey

13th to the 20th centuries. Works by such 19th-century French painters as Monet, Renoir, and Cézanne are especially popular. In the lower-floor galleries, you can see damaged paintings by great artists in addition to some excellent forgeries. Temporary displays include selected works from the museum's own collection as well as some of the world's top traveling exhibits.

The gallery offers special brochures, books, and educational events to focus attention on various aspects of its truly remarkable collection. Call ahead to take advantage of the regularly scheduled guided tours and guest lectures.

To the left of the main building is the **Sainsbury Wing,** which opened in 1991. Several designs for the building were rejected after Prince Charles called them "a carbuncle on the face of Trafalgar Square." The one that was finally accepted was submitted by American architect Robert Venturi.

The gallery's main entrance is flanked by two small statues. On the left is the:

5. **James II statue.** Created in 1686 by Grinling Gibbons, one of England's noted sculptors, this statue is widely regarded as one of the country's finest. James II ascended the throne in 1685 and quickly levied new—and unpopular—taxes. The king might have succeeded if he hadn't been so determined to restore Catholicism to England, a move that led to his deposition and forced exile in France, where he remained for the rest of his life. After James II died (1701), Benedictine monks kept his body embalmed in a French hearse for 92 years, waiting to see if the political and religious climate in England would change enough that the former king could be buried in his native land. This never came to pass, however, and James II was eventually buried at St-Germain.

On the right side of the gallery's entrance is the:

6. **George Washington statue,** a gift from the state of Virginia. It is a replica of the statue in that state's capitol building in Richmond. The gift also included two boxes of earth for the base of the statue, thereby ensuring that it would always stand on American soil.

Walk clockwise around Trafalgar Square to the:

7. **Church of St. Martin-in-the-Fields** (℡ 020/7766-1100), on the northeastern corner. This popular London church (which might be the finest work of James Gibb) is famous for its spire-topped classical portico—a style often copied in 18th-century America. Begun in 1722, the church is the burial site of several famous people, including furniture designer Thomas Chippendale and painter Sir Joshua Reynolds. After visiting the church, go downstairs to the **London Brass Rubbing Centre,** where, for a small fee, you'll be provided with materials and instructions for making rubbings of replicas of medieval church brasses. The church is open to visitors Monday to Saturday from 10am to 6pm, and Sunday from noon to 6pm.

On Monday and Tuesday at 1pm, the church usually holds free chamber-music concerts, often featuring works by well-known 19th-century composers. St. Martin's is also known for its exceptional choir; consider attending a full choral Sunday service.

Cross over to the square again and continue clockwise. At the southeast corner is a tiny cylindrical granite pillar, which is:

8. **London's smallest police station,** established in the 19th century as a secret observation post to enable the police to monitor marches and demonstrations held in the square. It barely accommodated one police officer and the hand-cranked phone that he could use to summon help from nearby Scotland Yard if necessary.

Go over the crossing; bear right over The Strand via the next crossing. Bear right and cross Charing Cross Road, pausing on the traffic island to look at the:

9. **Equestrian statue of Charles I,** which dates from 1633 and was designed by French sculptor Hubert Le Sueur. Because Charles viewed himself as a just, divinely ordained monarch, he wanted the statue to convey this image. Thus, though the king was only 5 feet tall, he specified that the statue depict him as 6 feet in height.

Following Charles's 1649 execution, the statue was given to a scrap-metal dealer with instructions to destroy it. The dealer made a fortune selling souvenirs allegedly made from the statue, which he had, in fact, buried in his garden. When the monarchy was restored in 1660, the dealer was able to present the undamaged statue to the new king, Charles II. It was placed here in 1765; the pedestal was designed by Sir Christopher Wren.

Proceed ahead onto Whitehall, cross to the right side, and walk for 1 block. On your right, you'll find two brightly suited guards on horseback. You've arrived at the:

10. **Horse Guards,** where you'll find soldiers of the Queen's Household Division. Two regiments of the Household Cavalry Regiment alternate their guard here. If the soldiers are wearing scarlet tunics, they belong to the Life Guards; if they're wearing blue tunics, they belong to the Blues and Royals. You can see one of the two regiments daily here from 10am to 4pm. There's a small, usually uncrowded changing-of-the-guard ceremony Monday to Saturday at 11am, and Sunday at 10am. The most interesting event is probably the guard inspection, when the commanding officer inspects the troops. The guard inspection takes place daily at 4pm.

Walk through the courtyard and under the Horse Guards Arch. Queen Victoria decreed that this arch should remain the official entrance to the royal palaces, even after the construction of Admiralty Arch. The parade ground on the other side of the arch is called:

11. **Horse Guards Parade.** This is the site of the Trooping the Colour, an impressive annual ceremony to celebrate the queen's official birthday. The queen is the colonel-in-chief of all seven regiments of the Household Division. The ceremony originated in the early days of land warfare, when military leaders used flags (colors) to rally their troops for battle. Because every soldier needed to be able to recognize his own unit's flag, it became the practice to carry (troop) the color down the ranks at the end of a day's march.

As you enter the Horse Guards Parade, look to your left. The building beyond the wall is the back of the prime minister's residence, **10 Downing St.** Your view from here is better than what is possible from the front (owing to security precautions).

Return to Whitehall and cross to the other side of the street. The building at the corner of Horse Guards Avenue is:

12. **Banqueting House,** the only remaining part of Whitehall Palace. Modeled by Inigo Jones on Sansovino's Library in Venice, the building was completed in 1622. London's first purely Renaissance building, Banqueting House was intended for receptions, banquets, and the-atrical performances. In 1635, Charles I commissioned Peter Paul Rubens to paint the ceilings, which glorified aspects of Charles's reign. These ceilings are breathtaking. Ironically, on January 30, 1649, Charles I was brought here to be executed. The king stepped out of an upstairs window onto a waiting scaffold and, in a steady voice, said, "I needed not have come here, and therefore I tell you (and I pray God it be not laid to your charge) that I am the martyr of the people." The king then placed his long hair under his cap, laid his neck on the chopping block, and stretched out his hands as a signal to the exe-cutioner to strike. His head was severed in a single blow and then held up to the crowds below, with the words "Behold the head of a traitor."

Cross Whitehall again and continue 1 block to the iron gates on the right side. This is:

13. **10 Downing Street,** the official residence of the British prime minister. No. 10 has been home to prime ministers since 1732, when it was acquired by the Crown and offered as a personal gift to First Lord of the Treasury Sir Robert Walpole, who would accept it only as an office. Unlike most of the government buildings on Whitehall, which were erected in the 19th century, the structures on Downing Street are small in scale, dating from 1680 to 1766. The street is named for Sir George Downing, a 17th-century Member of Parliament and a real-estate developer. Downing built this cul-de-sac of plain brick terrace houses around 1680; the only remaining houses are nos. 10, 11 (the office and home of the Chancellor of the Exchequer), and 12. Although they look small, the houses actually contain sizable rooms and offices.

Continue along Whitehall, which ends with a white obelisk in the center of the road, marking the beginning of Parliament Street. This obelisk is the:

14. **Cenotaph,** a tall, white monument of Portland stone that now commemorates the dead of both World Wars. Often surrounded by flowers and wreaths, it was designed by Sir Edwin Lutyens and placed here in 1920. The word *cenotaph* derives from the Greek words *kenos,* meaning "empty," and *taphos,* meaning "tomb." The monument's lines alternate between being slightly convex and concave, representing infinity. There are no religious symbols in the design; the only emblems are the flags of the three branches of the military and the standard of the merchant fleet.

Half a block ahead, turn right onto King Charles Street. At the far end, go down the steps and turn left to find the:

15. **Cabinet War Rooms,** (✆ 020/7930-6961), the government's underground World War II headquarters. Inside, you can see the Cabinet Room, the Map Room, Prime Minister Winston Churchill's emergency bedroom, and the Telephone Room (where calls to Franklin D. Roosevelt were made). All the rooms have been restored to their 1940s appearance—in fact, they've been so accurately recreated that there are even such details as an open pack of cigarettes on the table. The rooms are open daily from 10am to 5:30pm. There is an admission charge.

Return to Parliament Street and cross over to the:

🥤 **Take a Break**   **Red Lion Public House,** 48 Parliament St., frequented by Members of Parliament and other civil servants. In fact, so many MPs come here that the pub rings a "divisional bell" to call the lawmakers back to Parliament before a vote is taken. The food is above average, and the usual beers are available.

Look up at the second-floor window for a medallion depicting Charles Dickens. At age 11, Dickens came to this pub to enjoy a pint of beer. The hero of *David Copperfield,* at the same age, came here and asked the proprietor, "What's your strongest ale?" He was told, "Aye, that'll be the genuine Stunning Ale."

Exit the Red Lion, turn left onto Derby Gate, and look down the road at the red brick buildings of:

16. **New Scotland Yard,** the former home of England's top police force. When the foundation stone was laid in 1875, the intention was to build a lofty national opera house. A shortage of money stopped the project midway through, until 1878, when the Metropolitan Police proposed converting it into their headquarters. In an ironic twist, the granite used for the new building was quarried by convicts from Dartmoor Prison. Described by architect Norman Shaw as "a very constabulary kind of castle," the finished structure provided 140 offices for the elite group. Because there were no elevators, senior officers were assigned rooms on the lower floors, while lower-ranking police officers had the higher floors. In 1967, Scotland Yard left this building in favor of new headquarters on Victoria Street.

Return to Parliament Street and continue 1 block to:

17. **Parliament Square.** Laid out in the 1860s by Charles Barry, who also designed the new Houses of Parliament, this square was remodeled early in the 20th century, when its center was turned into a traffic island.

Turn left on Parliament Square, pass Westminster Underground Station, and cross over the busy Victoria Embankment via the traffic lights. Pause on arrival at Westminster Bridge where, on your left, you'll see the:

18. **Statue of Queen Boudicca,** depicting the ancient British queen (who died in A.D. 60) and her daughters in a war chariot. The sculpture was created by Thomas Hornicroft in the 1850s and unveiled here in 1902. It's believed that Prince Albert, the husband of Queen Victoria, lent his horses as models for this statue.

Now walk to the center of:

19. **Westminster Bridge,** a seven-arch cast-iron span that opened in 1750 and was rebuilt in 1862. The bridge's 26m (84 ft.) width was considered exceptional at the time.

From the center of the bridge, look left, toward the City of London. It was this view that in 1802 inspired William Wordsworth to write:

Earth has not anything to show more fair:
Dull would he be of soul who could pass by
A sight so touching in its majesty:
This City now doth like a garment wear
The beauty of the morning; silent, bare,
Ships, towers, domes, theatres, and temples lie
Open unto the fields, and to the sky;
All bright and glittering in the smokeless air.
—*"Upon Westminster Bridge"*

Admittedly, the view from the bridge has changed considerably since Wordsworth's day, though there are still some wonderful sights, including the ornate back side of the Houses of Parliament. The balcony with the green canopy is the river terrace of the House of Commons; the one with the red canopy is the river terrace of the House of Lords.

Return toward Parliament Square and stand at the foot of:

20. **Big Ben,** the world's most famous clock tower. Contrary to popular belief, Big Ben refers neither to the tower nor to the clock; it's the name of the largest bell in the chime. Hung in 1856, the bell might have been named for either Sir Benjamin Hall (the commissioner of works when the bell was hung) or Ben Caunt (a popular prizefighter of the era who, at age 42, fought in a match that lasted 60 rounds). Each of the tower's four 61m-/200-ft.-high clocks has a minute hand as large as a double-decker bus.

Walk clockwise around Parliament Square and stroll past the front of the:

21. **Houses of Parliament,** home of England's national legislature, which is made up of the **House of Commons** and the **House of Lords.** Officially known as the Royal Palace of St. Stephen at Westminster, the Houses are located on the site of a royal palace built by Edward the Confessor before the Norman Conquest of 1066. During Edward's reign, this stretch of land along the Thames was surrounded by water and known as Thorny Island, owing to the wild brambles that flourished here. The island was once a sort of pilgrimage site, celebrated for miracles believed to have taken place there; when Edward ascended

the throne, he chose this sacred spot to build the royal palace and church (Westminster Abbey). Later kings improved and enlarged the palace, which served as the official royal residence until 1512, when it was destroyed by fire.

The present Gothic-style building, with more than 1,000 rooms and 3.2km (2 miles) of corridors, was designed by Charles Barry and Augustus Pugin and was completed in 1860. On May 10, 1941, the House of Commons was destroyed by German bombs. It was rebuilt by Giles Gilbert Scott, the man who designed London's red telephone booths, but it remains small: Only 346 of its 650 members can sit at any one time, while the rest crowd around the door and the Speaker's Chair. The ruling party and the opposition sit facing each other, two sword lengths apart. This house holds the political power in Parliament, though those powers were greatly curtailed in 1911.

The House of Lords has seen a significant change in recent years, and the majority of its members are no longer hereditary peers but are rather appointed at the whim of the government. However, the opulently fur-nished chambers still have an almost sacrosanct feel, and the debates are still often as dull as ever, lacking as they do the drama and interest of those in the more important House of Commons. However, a visit here will enable you to see the pageantry of Parliament.

You may watch debates from the **Strangers' Galleries** of Parliament's two houses. This can be rather interesting and is especially exciting during debates over controversial topics.

The House of Commons is usually open to the public Mondays and Tuesdays 2:30pm to 10:30pm, Wednesdays 11:30am to 7:30pm, Thursdays 10:30am to 6:30pm, and Fridays 10:30am to 3:30pm. It should be noted, however, that the House doesn't sit every Friday. The House of Lords is generally open Monday to Thursday, beginning about 3pm, and on certain Fridays at the same time. To watch the debates in either of the houses, line up at St. Stephen's Entrance, just past the statue of Oliver Cromwell (see below).

Guided tours of The Houses of Parliament are operated in the months of August and September. There is a charge. Details can be obtained from the House of Commons Information Office (© **020/7219-4272**) or on the website (www.parliament.uk).

In the small garden in front of the Houses of Parliament is a:

22. **Statue of Oliver Cromwell,** a monument to England's only Lord Protector. Cromwell (1599–1658), who led the parliamentary armies during the Civil War that toppled Charles I, is depicted with a Bible in one hand and a sword in the other. When the statue was unveiled in 1899, it was vehemently criticized by Parliament's Irish representatives. Cromwell was hated in Ireland for his harsh policies, particularly the massacre of more than 30,000 men, women, and children in Drogheda, followed by a trail of death and devastation from Wexford to Connaught. Motivated by religious as well as political considerations, Cromwell awarded vast tracts of land to his loyal followers, leaving less than one ninth of Irish soil in Irish hands. Ultimately, Parliament refused to pay for the statue, and the prime minister at that time, Lord Rosebery, eventually paid for it himself.

Do Cromwell's eyes appear to be downcast, as though ashamed of something? Look across the street, directly opposite the statue. Above the small doorway of the church is a small **bust of Charles I,** the monarch who was beheaded at Cromwell's instigation.

The building behind the statue is:

23. **Westminster Hall,** the last remaining portion of the old Palace of Westminster. A majestic remnant of Romanesque and Gothic architecture, the hall was built by William Rufus (ca. 1056–1100), the son of William the Conqueror. Something of a boaster, William Rufus once referred to this hall as nothing—a mere bedchamber to his future projects (which in actuality never came to fruition).

Rebuilt from 1394 to 1402 for Richard II, the hall isn't much more than a large, rectangular banquet room, but it's noted for its magnificent oak hammer-beam roof. During the 15th and 16th centuries, some of England's best-known trials took place here, including those of Anne Boleyn and Sir Thomas More. Also tried here was Guy Fawkes, who conspired to blow up James I and the Houses of Parliament in the Gunpowder Plot of 1605. The 1649 trial of Charles I took place here as well before an extremely reluctant panel of judges. The king refused to accept the legality of the verdict or sentence, which read in part: "For all which treasons and crimes this Court doth adjudge that sets as a tyrant, traitor, murderer, and publique enemy to the good people of this nation shall be put to death by the severing of his head from his body."

Oliver Cromwell was proclaimed Lord Protector here, and, more recently, this is where Sir Winston Churchill's body lay in state. The criminal courts moved to the Royal Courts of Justice in the late 19th century, so Westminster Hall is now used only occasionally, primarily as a banquet hall for parliamentary functions. After a bomb killed a Member of Parliament (MP) in 1979, entrance to Westminster Hall became difficult. Tickets are available on a limited basis from your embassy.

Continue walking, keeping the Houses of Parliament to your left. Pass the Victoria Tower (through which the queen officially enters Parliament); a little way along, turn left through the gates into Victoria Tower Gardens. Follow the path as it bears right to arrive at the:

24. **Burghers of Calais,** by Auguste Rodin (1840–1917), commemorating the burghers' personal and perilous surrender of their city to Edward III in 1347. (Incidentally, Rodin was one of the greatest influences on British sculptors in the late 19th and early 20th centuries.)

Backtrack to the Victoria Tower, then cross the road at the crossing. The stone building set back in the sunken garden to your left is the:

25. **Jewel Tower** (© 020/7222-2219), built by Edward III about 1365 to house his personal wardrobe and valuables. This is one of only two surviving buildings from the original Palace of Westminster. It houses the "Parliament Past and Present" exhibition, illustrating how Parliament works.

Backtrack to the Old Palace Yard. Go past the ornate outer walls of Henry VII's chapel, and then turn left along the paved pathway that passes alongside:

26. **St. Margaret's Westminster,** a grand 16th-century church that's often mistaken for Westminster Abbey. Since 1614, St. Margaret's has been the parish church of the House of Commons, though it might be best known for its enormous East Window, which is brilliantly illuminated on bright days. This stained-glass masterpiece was presented to Henry VII by Ferdinand and Isabella of Spain to commemorate the marriage of their daughter, Catherine of Aragon, to Henry VII's eldest son, Arthur. The stained-glass gift was intended for Westminster Abbey, but by the time it arrived here from Spain, Arthur had died and his brother, Henry VIII, had already married Catherine.

   Exit St. Margaret's via the main door and walk a few steps to:

27. **Westminster Abbey** (© 020/7222-5152). This famed Benedictine abbey, which housed a community of monks as early as A.D. 750, was called Westminster (West Monastery) because of its location west of the city. In 1052, Edward the Confessor initiated construction of the present building; it was consecrated in 1065. William the Conqueror was crowned at the abbey in 1066, and most British monarchs have continued to be crowned here. When not in use, the Coronation Chair (built in 1300) sits behind the abbey's High Altar. Many British monarchs have been married and buried in the abbey as well. And, of course, in September 1997, the abbey was the site of the funeral service for the adored Diana, Princess of Wales.

   Poets' Corner is the final resting place of some of Britain's most famous bards, including Geoffrey Chaucer, Robert Browning, and Alfred, Lord Tennyson. The **Henry VII Chapel,** with its architectural extravagances and exquisite carvings, will take your breath away.

   The abbey is open Monday to Saturday from 9:30am to 5pm. The Royal Chapels are open Monday, Tuesday, Thursday, and Friday from 9am to 4:45pm; Wednesday from 9am to 8pm; and Saturday from 9am to 2pm and 3:30 to 5:45pm. There is an admission charge. Comprehensive "Super Tours" condense the abbey's 900-year history into 1½ hours; though these tours are expensive, many believe that they're worth it.

Exit right from Westminster Abbey and go right onto Victoria Street. Walk to the pedestrian crossing and go straight over it into **Parliament Square.** Walking clockwise, you'll notice that the square is surrounded by statues. In fact, the square boasts the greatest concentration of outdoor sculptures in the city. Cross to the interior garden of Parliament Square. The statue nearest to you in the garden is of:

Sir Robert Peel, former prime minister and founder of London's Metropolitan Police Force, hence their nickname "Bobbies." In a House of Commons speech lasting over 4 hours, Peel introduced a bill for Catholic emancipation based on equality of civil rights. As he moved from point to point, his audience cheered so loudly that they could be heard in Westminster Hall. The 1876 statue depicts Peel wearing a frock coat. Standing next to Peel, with his back toward you, is:

Benjamin Disraeli, England's first prime minister of Jewish ancestry. Disraeli was said to have delighted in shocking people, a trait that led to hundreds of exaggerated stories about his behavior. One woman's claim that the prime minister appeared at a party wearing green velvet trousers and a black satin shirt became so popular that Disraeli himself wrote to a London newspaper editor to deny having ever owned a pair of green trousers in his life. This statue was unveiled in 1883, on the second anniversary of Disraeli's death. Behind Disraeli, across the street, is:

Abraham Lincoln, the only non-British individual represented on the square. This monument, a gift from the city of Chicago, is an exact replica of the one in Lincoln Park.

In the northwest corner of Parliament Square, standing next to the statue of Disraeli, is the:

14th Earl of Derby (Edward Stanley). Four pediment bronze reliefs depict highlights of the earl's career: as a member of the House of Commons, as chancellor of the University of Oxford, as a participant in the Famine Relief Committee in Manchester, and as part of the Cabinet Council. Standing to Derby's right is:

Viscount Palmerston. Secretary of War for nearly twenty years, Palmerston was known for his nonpartisan politics. Tories thought him too Whiggish, and Whigs suspected him of Toryism. He was sympathetic to the Greek struggle for independence and consistently advocated and voted for Catholic emancipation, which he predicted "would give peace to Ireland." The next statue along is:

Gen. Jan Smuts, who appears to be ice-skating. An expert in early guerrilla warfare, Smuts commanded the Boer forces in the Second South African War (the Boer War). He later commanded the South African forces in World War I and held many South African government posts, including that of prime minister.

The final statue, nearest the Houses of Parliament, is:

Sir Winston Churchill, one of Britain's greatest statesmen. The statue was created by Ivor Roberts-Jones in 1973 and shows Churchill leaning on a stick, bulldog fashion, looking across the street toward the Houses of Parliament.

Cross Parliament Square to the corner of Parliament Street, where you will find the underpass that leads into Westminster Underground Station.

St. James's

Start: Green Park Underground Station.
Finish: Green Park Underground Station.
Time: Two hours.
Best Time: Monday to Saturday from 9:30am to 5pm.
Worst Time: Sundays, when shops are closed.

T his small corner of London, nestled between Green Park and St. James's Park, has long been favored by the upper classes. The St. James's area sprang up around the Royal Palace of Henry VIII. Believing that it would be advantageous to be close to power, the wealthy erected splendid homes for themselves near the palace. St. James's heyday was in the 18th and 19th centuries, when most of the houses, shops, and clubs were built, many with riches acquired throughout the empire.

The British class system is an outgrowth of the nation's past. The Royal Family remains a potent symbol of the importance that many British attach to birth. More than three quarters of the members of the House of Lords are hereditary peers, meaning that they inherit their seats as a birthright. Even today, a number of England's nobility are wealthy simply because they own land that has been passed down for generations—land that was given to their ancestors by a king or queen hundreds of years ago. Many of the buildings on this tour that might seem unremarkable for their architecture are actually worth seeing for the culture and history that they represent.

• • • • • • • • • • • • • • • • •

Leave Green Park Underground Station via the Buckingham Palace/Ritz Hotel exit. Turn right on Piccadilly and walk toward the Ritz. Just after the telephone boxes, turn right and go through the iron gates onto an unmarked pedestrian walkway called Queen's Walk. On your right is:

1. **Green Park,** owned by the Crown estate and so named because it contains no flower beds. Although the reason for this lack of flowers isn't precisely known, one popular story has it that Charles II was walking here one day with his entourage when he announced that he planned to pick a flower to give to the most beautiful lady present. When he gave it to a milkmaid from the local dairy, Queen Catherine became so enraged that she ordered all the park's flowers removed. Over the years, Green Park has been the setting for duels, balloon ascents, and various other events. In 1749, to celebrate the Treaty of Aix-la-Chapelle (which ended the War of Austrian Succession), a spectacular fireworks display was arranged and Handel composed his "Music for the Royal Fireworks." Green Park is popular today with picnickers, strollers, and British sun-worshipers (when the sun is out).

   Continue down Queen's Walk and notice the still-functioning gas lamps lining the path. After the fifth lamp, turn left down the passage that runs beneath several residential buildings (which, incidentally, are some of London's most expensive apartments). After emerging on the other side, turn right. Just opposite, you'll see the:

2. **Stafford Hotel,** 16–18 St. James's Place, favored by American humorist James Thurber since his first stay in 1955. Thurber, who is perhaps best known for his short story "The Secret Life of Walter Mitty," was admired in England and relished the attention he received. He believed that there was something about the country that enabled writers to achieve a ripe old age. By contrast, he

St. James's

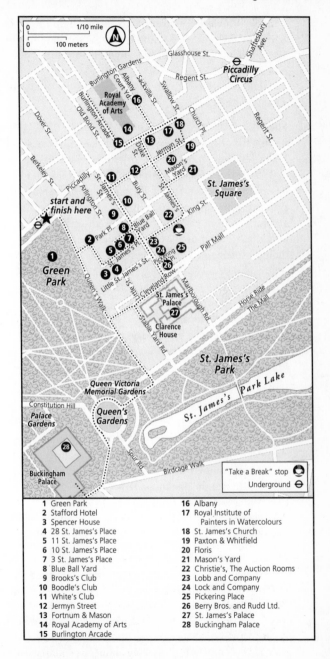

1 Green Park	**16** Albany
2 Stafford Hotel	**17** Royal Institute of
3 Spencer House	Painters in Watercolours
4 28 St. James's Place	**18** St. James's Church
5 11 St. James's Place	**19** Paxton & Whitfield
6 10 St. James's Place	**20** Floris
7 3 St. James's Place	**21** Mason's Yard
8 Blue Ball Yard	**22** Christie's, The Auction Rooms
9 Brooks's Club	**23** Lobb and Company
10 Boodle's Club	**24** Lock and Company
11 White's Club	**25** Pickering Place
12 Jermyn Street	**26** Berry Bros. and Rudd Ltd.
13 Fortnum & Mason	**27** St. James's Palace
14 Royal Academy of Arts	**28** Buckingham Palace
15 Burlington Arcade	

remarked, most male writers in America didn't seem to live past the age of 60, and those who did live beyond that age, he claimed, no longer had anything to say (but often said it anyway).

Continue 1 block to the grand house at the end of the street, which is:

3. **Spencer House,** 27 St. James's Place (© **020/7409-0526**), the ancestral home of the late Diana, Princess of Wales. The house, built for Earl John Spencer, was begun in 1765 by John Vardy, a pupil of William Kent, and was completed by James Stuart after the shell had been constructed. The working gas lamps and torch extinguishers around the front door are typical of an earlier age. The house hasn't been used as a private residence since 1927, though it remained the property of the trustees of the eighth Earl Spencer's marriage settlement. In the 1980s, Jacob Rothschild took over the lease and had the building restored as a favor to Diana. Now operated by the Spencer Trust, it is used primarily for private functions. The house is open to the public on Sundays, from 11am to 4:45pm. A guided tour is scheduled every 30 minutes. There is an admission charge.

The building next door to the left is:

4. **28 St. James's Place,** the former home of William Huskisson. A treasurer of the British navy in the early 19th century, and arch-rival of the Duke of Wellington, Huskisson might best be remembered as the first person to be fatally injured by a steam-powered train; the accident occurred at the opening ceremony for the Liverpool–Manchester railway in 1830.

Continue along St. James's Place. On your left, you'll find:

5. **11 St. James's Place,** the former home of Robert Cruikshank, one of London's most beloved satirical cartoonists. In the early 19th century, Cruikshank and his brother George created the cartoon characters Tom and Jerry—two stylish and bawdy young men who were featured in a series of engravings called "Life in London" from 1820 to 1821. The cartoons, which were popular in

both England and America, were the model for today's popular and always-at-war animated cat and mouse.

Next door you'll see:

6. **10 St. James's Place,** where writer Oscar Wilde kept an apartment in the 1890s. It was here that Wilde met with several young men who testified against him at his "gross indecency" trial in 1895. (For more information on Wilde, see stop 16 in Walking Tour 10, p. 144.)

A few doors farther down the street is:

7. **3 St. James's Place,** which was occupied by composer Frédéric Chopin (1810–49) for a month in 1848. Chopin was living here when he gave his last public performance—at London's Guildhall.

At the end of St. James's Place, turn left onto St. James's Street, walk a few yards, and turn left again into:

8. **Blue Ball Yard,** a delightful cobblestone courtyard from 1741. Named for the Blue Ball Inn that once stood here, the yard is now the setting for some of London's most picturesque residences. The two-story buildings here, which now house guest rooms for the Stafford Hotel, were once used as stables; look for the silhouetted images of horses' heads that hang above names such as Pharlap and Copenhagen.

Return to St. James's Street, turn left, and cross Park Place. The next couple of blocks along St. James's Street are some of the swankiest in London (if not the world). Located here are some of London's most exclusive gentlemen's clubs. For centuries, these bastions of privilege have provided lodging, food, drink, and good company for the well-to-do. Women aren't permitted on the premises of most of these clubs, and aspiring members might wait many years to be accepted into them. None of these clubs displays its name—that would only encourage attention from the general public, including sightseers (who aren't permitted inside anyway).

The ornate building on the far left corner of St. James's Street and Park Place is:

9. **Brooks' Club,** 60 St. James's St. This 1778 building was constructed for the Whig politicians who supported the

American revolutionaries. The Whigs, who viewed the revolutionaries as fellow Englishmen, also wanted to escape the rule of George III. One of the club's objectives was to collect money for "the widows, orphans, and aged parents of our beloved American fellow-subjects, who, faithful to the character of Englishmen, preferring death to slavery, were for that reason only inhumanly murdered by the king's troops at or near Lexington and Concord."

With your back toward Brooks,' look across the street at the white building. This is:

10. **Boodle's Club,** 28 St. James's St. This 1775 building is named after one of its earliest managers, Edward Boodle, a man who squandered his large inheritance and delighted in teaching young men to drink heavily. It's not surprising that the club quickly acquired a reputation for intense gambling and good food. Past members have included historian Edward Gibbon (author of *The Decline and Fall of the Roman Empire*), abolitionist William Wilberforce, socialite George Bryan ("Beau") Brummell, and the Duke of Wellington. The room on the third floor, to the left of the Venetian window, is the "undress dining room," where members can dine in informal clothes. Behind the Venetian window is the club's main salon, which is 1½ stories high.

Continue along St. James's, cross at the pedestrian crossing, bear left, and cross Jermyn Street to arrive at the white stone building, the second structure on the block. This is:

11. **White's Club,** 37–38 St. James's St., the oldest and grandest of the St. James's gentlemen's clubs. This club, founded in 1693, was originally established on the site of White's Chocolate House, a coffeehouse that opened that same year. The club moved to its current site in the late 18th century.

The club quickly acquired a reputation for around-the-clock gambling; as one popular gentlemen's magazine noted: "There is nothing, however trivial or ridiculous, which is not capable of producing a bet." One 1750 report tells of a man who happened to collapse near the door of this club; he was carried upstairs and immediately became the object of bets as to whether he was dead! One rainy day, it's said Lord Arlington bet £3,000 on which of two drops of rain would reach the bottom of a windowpane first. Bets were placed on births, deaths, marriages, public events, and politics—almost anything that came up in conversation or caused an argument.

The club has a long conservative history and still claims many political Tories as members. Prince Charles is affiliated with this club. When the Labour political leader Aneurin Bevan, who had once described all Tories as "lower than vermin," dined here in 1950, he was kicked in the bottom by a member (who was then forced to resign).

Walk two doors back on St. James's Street and turn left onto:

12. **Jermyn Street,** one of the world's most expensive shopping streets. The small stores lining the street are famous for their long-standing service to upper-class and royal clients. Several display Royal Warrants above their front doors—coats of arms given to merchants who provide goods to members of the Royal Family. On your right, the colorful shop front of the royal shirtmakers **Turnbull & Asser,** 71–72 Jermyn St., is especially noteworthy, as is **Taylor of Old Bond Street,** 74 Jermyn St., a 19th century–era beauty salon specializing in herbal remedies and aromatherapy.

Take the first left onto Duke Street St. James's. The lime-colored building on your right is:

13. **Fortnum & Mason,** 181 Piccadilly (℡ 020/7734-8040), the royal grocers. Enter the store at the Duke Street entrance to be greeted by one of the formally attired attendants.

Fortnum's, as it's affectionately called, was started by William Fortnum, a footman in Queen Anne's household. Because part of his job entailed replenishing the royal candelabras, Fortnum supplemented his income by selling the queen's partially used candles. When he retired in 1707, Fortnum opened this upscale grocery store with his friend Hugh Mason. It was an immediate success, and by 1788 the shop had become world famous, shipping preserved foods and traditional specialties to English military, diplomatic, and other personnel overseas. Visitors to London's Great Exhibition of 1851—the first World's Fair—came to Fortnum's to marvel at the exotic fruits and prepared foods and to buy picnic hampers (which are still a popular purchase today).

On June 16, 1886, a smartly dressed American came to Fortnum's to meet with the head of grocery purchasing. Introducing himself as "a food merchant from Pittsburgh," the American gave Fortnum's grocer his first taste of horseradish, chili sauce, and tomato ketchup. Excited by these new tastes, the grocer enthusiastically said, "I think, Mr. Heinz, we will take them all." H. J. Heinz had arrived.

Exit Fortnum's main doors onto Piccadilly and look up at the glockenspiel clock above the front entrance. If you're lucky enough to be here on the hour, you'll hear the clock chime the "Eton Boat Song," as the doors swing open to reveal little figures depicting Mr. Fortnum and Mr. Mason.

With your back to Fortnum & Mason, cross Piccadilly. Piccadilly is one of the city's major commercial thorough-fares; its name derives from the ornate "piccadill" collars worn by fashionable men in the 17th century.

The large building to your right is the:

14. **Royal Academy of Arts,** Burlington House, Piccadilly (© 020/7439-4996), the last of half a dozen upper-class mansions that lined Piccadilly in the mid–17th century. Founded in 1768, the Royal Academy is the oldest so-ciety in England dedicated exclusively to the fine arts. Works by Reynolds, Turner, Gainsborough, Constable, and Stubbs are displayed here. Michelangelo's *Madonna and Child with the Infant St. John* is also here; it's one of only four of the master's sculptures outside Italy. The Academy, which moved to this site in 1868, is also well known for its annual summer exhibition, where contem-porary works are shown and (often) sold. The galleries are open Monday to Saturday from 10am to 6pm, and there's an admission charge.

To the left of the Royal Academy is the:

15. **Burlington Arcade,** one of the world's oldest shopping malls. The arcade was designed by Samuel Ware and built

in 1819 by Lord George Cavendish "for the gratification of the public and to give employment to Industrious females." Lord Cavendish lived next door in Burlington House and reputedly built the arcade to stop bawdy Londoners from throwing oyster shells into his garden.

Tailcoated watchmen, called beadles, continue to enforce the arcade's original code of behavior, making sure that visitors don't run, shout, sing, hum, or whistle.

Backtrack to Piccadilly and turn left. Walk past Burlington House and take the first left turn into the courtyard of the:

16. **Albany,** a 1770 Georgian apartment building that's one of London's most prestigious addresses. Built for the 1st Viscount Melbourne, the Albany was sold in 1802 to a young developer named Alexander Copland, who commissioned architect Henry Holland to convert the building into flats for single young men—bachelor apartments. Many authors, playwrights, and poets have lived here, including Graham Greene, Aldous Huxley, J. B. Priestly, and Lord Byron. (Even Oscar Wilde's fictitious Jack Worthing—who was "Jack" in the country but "Ernest" in town—lived at the Albany, as his calling card stated in *The Importance of Being Earnest.*) During her nine-month infatuation with Lord Byron, Lady Caroline Lamb once managed to enter Byron's Albany apartment disguised as a pageboy. She didn't find Byron at home, but she wrote "Remember me" on the flyleaf of one of his books; Byron was so upset by this invasion of his privacy that he penned a poem ending with these words:

> Remember thee! Aye doubt it not,
> Thy husband too shall think of thee,
> By neither shall thou be forgot,
> Thou false to him, thou fiend to me!

Continue down Piccadilly and look across the street at the former premises of the:

17. **Royal Institute of Painters in Watercolours,** 195 Piccadilly (above Princes Arcade), the former headquarters of the British School of Watercolour Painting. The school opened in 1831, and this building was constructed specifically for its use in 1882. Between every window

you can see busts of those who founded the school, including that of J. M. W. Turner. When the school's lease on this building expired in 1970, it moved to Pall Mall.

Cross Piccadilly at the traffic light and enter the courtyard of:

18. **St. James's Church,** 197 Piccadilly (℡ 020/7734-4511), a postwar reconstruction of one of Sir Christopher Wren's loveliest churches. Consecrated in 1684 and known as the Visitors Church, St. James's is indeed one of the city's most visitor-friendly chapels. The staff is affable, and the atmosphere is welcoming.

To the right of the entrance is an old **American catalpa tree** and a plaque reading: "When tired or sad an Amerindian will hug a tree to get in touch with earth's energy—why not you?" Across from the tree, on the church wall, is a pulpit formerly used for outdoor noontime sermons. Today, the noise from cars on Piccadilly would probably make this impractical.

Enter St. James's Church and turn left into the main chapel. The interior of this church is exceptionally elegant; Corinthian columns support splendid barrel vaults decorated with ornate plasterwork. In 1684, diarist John Evelyn expressed his view that "there was no altar anywhere in England, nor has there been any abroad more handsomely adorned."

The marble **font** at the rear-left corner of the chapel is the church's greatest prize. Created by Grinling Gibbons, London's most famous Stuart-era sculptor, the intricate stem represents Adam and Eve standing on either side of the Tree of Life. Poet William Blake, among others, was baptized here.

The large **organ** at the back of the church was made in 1685 for James II's Chapel Royal in nearby Whitehall and given to St. James's in 1691. Its case was carved by Grinling Gibbons. Two British composers, John Blow and Henry Purcell, reportedly played the organ soon after its installation. When it was being repaired in 1852, a miniature coffin containing a bird was discovered inside the instrument.

Near the fourth window on the left side of the church is a **plaque** honoring Sir Richard Croft, a 19th-century royal physician. His story is rather tragic. In 1817, Croft was caring for the pregnant Princess Charlotte—the only child of the Prince Regent. Because of pregnancy-related complications, Croft decided to bleed the princess and permit her very little food, hoping that this would cure her of a "morbid excess of animal spirits." After being in labor for 50 hours, Charlotte gave birth to a stillborn baby and died a few hours later. Although the Prince Regent published a kindly tribute to Croft, the physician's reputation was ruined. In February 1818, Croft was asked to care for another pregnant woman whose symptoms resembled those of Princess Charlotte. Before the birth, however, the doctor found a pistol hanging on the wall of the woman's house and shot himself.

Leave the church via the exit located directly opposite the door you entered. Go right along Jermyn Street until you reach:

19. **Paxton & Whitfield,** 93 Jermyn St. (✆ **020/7930-0259**), a store known for its cheeses and its terrific meat and fruit pies.

A few doors down is:

20. **Floris,** 89 Jermyn St. (✆ **020/7930-2885**), the city's most exclusive perfumery, which has been making its wealthy clients smell nice since 1810. Notice the almost garishly large Royal Warrant above the window. This old shop is something of a scent museum, and you might enjoy going in to see the delightful old display cases.

Continue to the traffic lights and turn left onto Duke Street St. James's. Just past the Cavendish Hotel, turn left into:

21. **Mason's Yard,** a small square with some interesting associations. No. 6 Mason's Yard, on the left, was once the site of the Indica Art Gallery, a center for the 1960s avant-garde movement. Shareholders in the gallery included Beatles Paul McCartney and John Lennon. In fact, it was here that John Lennon and Yoko Ono first met.

Diagonally across the courtyard, to your left, is the **Directors Lodge Club,** 13 Mason's Yard. Now a hostess bar for men, this was formerly the site of a bar called the "Scotch of St. James," a favorite haunt of the Beatles, the

Rolling Stones, and others during the 1960s. Some say that Jimi Hendrix was "discovered" here.

Retrace your footsteps, and go left along Duke Street St. James's, past upscale art galleries; after 1 block, turn right onto King Street, where on your right is:

22. **Christie's, The Auction Rooms,** 8 King St. (© 020/ 7839-9060), one of the world's best-known fine-art auctioneers. Established in 1766 by James Christie, a former navy midshipman, the establishment was moved to this location by the founder's son, James Jr., in 1823.

Opposite the auction house is the:

Take a Break Golden Lion Pub, 25 King St. This pub has strong theatrical connections: The monstrous modern office block on the opposite side of the alleyway from the pub stands on the site of the St. James's Theatre. It was here that Oscar Wilde's first major success as a playwright, *Lady Windermere's Fan,* was first performed in 1892. Taking his curtain call on opening night, Wilde delighted the audience by thanking them for having the good taste and intelligence to appreciate his play! The theater was demolished in 1957, despite a vigorous protest campaign orchestrated by Laurence Olivier and Vivien Leigh. The walls of the Golden Lion Pub are adorned with photographs of the actors who performed at the theater, as well as playbills from productions staged there. Good pub lunches are served with Tetley, Burton, and other English ales, and each month there's a guest beer.

Walk 1 block and turn left onto St. James's Street. Half a block down on your left is:

23. **Lobb and Company,** 9 St. James's St. (© 020/7930-5849), shoe- and bootmakers to the royals and the gentry. From left to right, the Royal Warrants above the door are from Queen Elizabeth, the Duke of Edinburgh, and the Prince of Wales. Inside, you can usually see a variety of wooden moldings of clients' feet used for custom-made shoes. Hidden in the shop's vaults are centuries-old moldings as well as contemporary castings of famous royal feet, including those of Prince Charles, the late Princess Diana, Queen Elizabeth, and Prince Philip.

A few doors down is:

24. **Lock and Company,** 6 St. James's St. (℃ 020/7930-
5849). Located at these premises since 1764, this hat
maker has covered some of the world's most important
heads: Lord Nelson ordered a hat from Lock with a built-
in eye patch, while the Duke of Wellington bought from
Lock the famous plumed hat that he wore at the Battle of
Waterloo. It's said that the top hat was designed here in
1797; its height caused such a furor that the first wearer
was arrested and fined £50 for "going about in a manner
calculated to frighten timid people." In 1850, William
Coke, a gamekeeper, ordered from Lock a hard, domed
hat for protection while chasing poachers. Produced by
Thomas and William Bowler, Lock's chief suppliers, the
hat became known worldwide as a "bowler." Around St.
James's, however, the hat was called a "coke," after the
man who had ordered it.

Continue down St. James's Street. The narrow alleyway three doors down on your left is:

25. **Pickering Place,** home of the Texas Legation from 1842
to 1845. Before Texas became a U.S. state, the Republic
of Texas had its own diplomatic mission in Britain; a lone
star on the wall of the alley commemorates the delegation's headquarters.

Enter the alley and walk to the delightfully quiet
enclosed courtyard. The buildings surrounding you were
constructed in the 1730s by William Pickering. Although
you can't see them, you're standing over a series of cellars
where Louis-Napoléon Bonaparte, later to become
Napoléon III, is rumored to have plotted his return to
France during his exile in the 1840s.

Return to St. James's Street; the building immediately
to your left is:

26. **Berry Bros. and Rudd Ltd.,** 3 St. James's St. (℃ 020/
7396-9600), wine and spirit merchants with Royal
Warrants. If you drink Cutty Sark whisky, you know that
the Berry Bros. name appears on each bottle. Notice the
18th-century wooden shop front, which was heavily
scratched by stones churned up by the wheels of passing
carriages. Founded in 1696, Berry Bros. began as a

grocery store; inside is a huge set of scales that was brought in for weighing coffee. Uncommon in their time, the scales became popular with customers, who often weighed themselves on them. Over the past 300 years or so, nearly 30,000 local people have weighed themselves here, and their weights have been recorded in large ledgers. In addition to the weights of Lord Byron, Lord Nelson, and Lady Hamilton, you can find the recorded weights of William IV (189 lbs., in boots); Queen Victoria's father, the Duke of Kent (232 lbs.); and others. The 4th Baron Rivers recorded his weight on almost 500 occasions; his entry for July 27, 1864, reads: "12 stone 4 lbs. at 1.30; 12 stone 5 lbs. at 2pm after two chops and a pint of sherry." (*Note:* 1 stone = 14 lbs.)

Walk half a block to the end of St. James's Street, which terminates at:

27. **St. James's Palace.** This palace, which dates from the reign of Henry VIII (1509–1547), was the main seat of England's kings and queens for more than 300 years, until Queen Victoria moved the royal residence to Buckingham Palace in 1837. It was in the chapel here that the body of Princess Diana lay in September 1997, awaiting her funeral, while thousands of people stood in line for hours to sign books of condolence.

Named for a convent that once stood on this site, St. James's Palace is today the headquarters of the Yeomen of the Guard and contains the Lord Chamberlain's office. Until recently, the ceremoniously garbed sentries who guard the front gate carried only swords. However, threats from the Irish Republican Army and others prompted a switch to bayoneted machine guns. By tradition, the stone-faced sentries aren't supposed to talk—but feel free to take their pictures.

Turn right at the palace, walk to Cleveland Row, and turn left onto Stable Yard Road. Pause at the security barrier to look at **Clarence House,** formerly the home of the late Her Majesty Queen Elizabeth, the Queen Mother; and now the home of Prince Charles and Camilla, Duchess of Cornwall. Backtrack on Stable Yard Road to Cleveland Row and turn left. Take the small Milk Maid's

Passage, located in the far right corner, to Queen's Walk. Turn left and walk down to The Mall, then turn right to:

28. **Buckingham Palace** (© 020/7839-1377), the home of Elizabeth II and Prince Philip. Originally owned by the Duke of Buckingham, this building was acquired by King George III in 1762. Over the next 75 years, architects John Nash and Edward Blore enlarged and renovated the palace. The expansion was still not finished when Queen Victoria moved into the building in 1837—successive modifications have enlarged the palace to almost 600 rooms. However, the popularity of the palace isn't due to its age or its architecture—it's neither old nor spectacular. Instead, as home to one of the world's few remaining celebrated monarchs, the building is of symbolic interest. Although the public view is of the rather plain neo-Georgian east front (added by Sir Aston Webb in 1913), the best view might be from the back, where the queen's famous garden parties are held.

The **Changing of the Guard** ceremony, performed by five rotating regiments of the Queen's Foot Guards, is held here daily at 11:30am from April to July, and on alternate days at 11:30am from August to March. (The ceremony isn't held during bad weather or at the time of major state events.)

The ceremony actually begins at 11am, when the St. James's Palace detachment of the Old Guard assembles in Friary Court at St. James's Palace. The captain of the Queen's Guard performs an inspection, then the drummers beat the call "The point of war," and the flag is brought on. With this done, the corps of drummers leads the way and the St. James's detachment marches off via The Mall to Buckingham Palace.

Meanwhile, the Buckingham Palace detachment of the Old Guard has fallen in and been inspected. It's joined by the St. James's Old Guard, which assembles to the right in the forecourt of Buckingham Palace.

At 11:30am, the New Guard approaches the palace from Birdcage Walk, enters the grounds via the north center gate, marches to a central position, and executes a left-form, halting in front of the Old Guard.

As the two groups stand facing each other, the captains of the Guard march toward each other and perform the ceremony of handing over the palace keys. Symbolically, the responsibility for the security of the palace has now passed from the Old to the New Guard. At 12:05pm, the Old Guard exits the palace grounds via the center gate and marches back to the barracks.

Guided tours of the public rooms at Buckingham Palace are available during August and September (when the Royal Family is away for holidays). There's an admission charge.

Return to Queen's Walk and follow it for the whole length; then turn left onto Piccadilly. Half a block along, on the left, is Green Park Underground Station.

The East End

Start: Whitechapel Underground Station.

Finish: Aldgate East Underground Station.

Time: 2 hours, moderately paced.

Best Time: Monday to Friday until 4pm.

Worst Time: Saturdays, Sundays, and evenings after 5pm.

The East End, an ill-defined area hugging the City of London's eastern edge, encompasses two adjacent territories: Whitechapel and Spitalfields. The East End has long been one of London's poorest areas. In the past, it was considered undesirable because the prevailing winds and the west-to-east flow of the Thames carried diseases from the city and the hamlets to the west. Living on the "wrong" side of the city was dangerous indeed.

The East End has a long history as a home for newly arrived immigrants, first from Ireland and the Continent, and in more recent years from the Indian subcontinent and the Caribbean. In the early 1900s, the area was also home to most of England's Jewish population—by 1914, almost 90% of England's Jews lived in Spitalfields, Whitechapel, and St. George's, to the east.

Spitalfields was once England's silk-weaving center, established in the 16th and 17th centuries by French and Flemish weavers. By the end of the 18th century, about 17,000 looms were in operation, making weaving one of the largest businesses in the East End. Weaving has faded from the East End, but there are many reminders of the area's history.

The East End's most notorious connection is with Jack the Ripper, whose infamous series of still-unsolved murders took place in Whitechapel in 1888.

•••••••••••••••••

Exit Whitechapel Underground Station and turn right along Whitechapel Road. Six doors along, on the right, is:

1. **259 Whitechapel Road.** In November 1884, Joseph Merrick (1862–1890), the so-called "Elephant Man," was displayed here in a freak show as the "Deadly Fruit of Original Sin." Dr. Frederick Treves (1853–1923), a surgeon at the London Hospital (which stands on the opposite side of Whitechapel Road), came to view Merrick on display at this vacant greengrocer's shop. The doctor was shocked by the "degraded or perverted version of a human being [that] this lone figure displayed . . ." Treves described how the "most striking feature about him [Merrick] was his enormous and misshapened head. From the brow there projected a huge bony mass like a loaf, while from the back of his head hung a bag of spongy, fungous-looking skin . . . From the upper jaw there projected another mass of bone. It protruded from the mouth like a pink stump." It was this growth from the jaw that earned Merrick the moniker "Elephant Man." Treves was so moved by the plight of this poor unfortunate that he befriended him and, in 1886, moved him into the London Hospital, where he lived until his death in April 1890.

   With your back to number 259, pass through the busy and lively street market that fills Whitechapel Road most days of the week. This market began in the 1850s when the road was widened. In its early days, the merchants were mostly immigrants who had fled Ireland during the potato famine of 1845–48. By the end of the 19th century, the majority of stall holders were Jewish. Today, the bulk of the merchants are Asian.

Cross Whitechapel Road via the pedestrian crossing, heading towards the clearly discernable:

2. **Royal London Hospital.** Founded in 1747 in the City of London, the hospital moved to this site in 1757. Its medical college opened in 1785 and has the distinction of being England's first hospital-based medical school. The hospital continued to expand throughout the 19th century, and two pavilion wings, added in the 1860s and 1870s, made it the largest hospital in the country at the time, with 650 beds.

In 1866, Thomas John Barnardo came to study medicine at the hospital, his ultimate intention being to become a missionary. However, he was so appalled by the number of homeless children that he found sleeping on the area's streets that he changed his plans and became a part-time teacher in one of the neighborhood's "ragged schools." The knowledge he acquired about the lifestyle and plight of the area's children led him to establish the East End Juvenile Mission in 1868. Two years later, Barnardo founded his first home for homeless children; the sign over its door read: NO DESTITUTE BOY OR GIRL EVER REFUSED ADMISSION. So began "Dr. Barnardo's Homes," which still provide both residential and nonresidential care for thousands of orphaned and destitute children throughout the world.

Turn right in front of the Royal London Hospital, passing the bus stop and phone box. Then turn left through the gates and pass the hospital's Alexandra Wing. Proceed along Turner Street, passing the Good Samaritan Public House on the right, and take a left onto Newark Street. Keep going straight until you reach:

3. **The Museum and Archives of the Royal London Hospital,** Newark Street (℃ **020/7377-7608**). This tiny museum recounts the history of the Royal London Hospital through displays, photographs, and text. Among the exhibits are photographs of Joseph Merrick (the "Elephant Man"), along with the peaked cap and veil that he wore over his head to protect himself from the prying eyes of curious bystanders when he ventured out in public. Another display relates the history of forensic science

at the hospital, featuring photographs and illustrations associated with the Jack the Ripper Murders, which took place in the surrounding area in the fall of 1888. The Museum is open Monday to Friday from 10am to 4:30pm. Admission is free.

Backtrack to the Good Samaritan Pub, and turn left along Stepney Way. Walk into Fieldgate Street. The looming, oppressive-looking building that dominates the right side of the street is:

4. **Tower House,** built in 1902 to provide accommodation for 816 single, homeless men. Gazing up at its soaring walls, punctured by a seemingly endless number of dark, tiny windows, and crowned by gloomy turrets, it is easy to see why this building was known by locals and residents alike as the "Monster Doss House." At the time of writing, the building is converted into comfortable apartments.

Keep traveling along Fieldgate Street until you see the:

5. **East London Mosque,** its golden glass-fiber dome making for a truly eye-catching landmark on this otherwise uneventful section of the walk.

On arrival at the junction of Fieldgate Street and Plumber's Row, cross diagonally right over the latter to arrive at:

6. **Whitechapel Bell Foundry,** 324 Whitechapel Rd. (© 020/7247-2599), which has been casting bells since 1570 (and at this location since 1738). Some of the world's most famous bells have been cast here, including Big Ben, Westminster Abbey's bells, and America's original Liberty Bell. There is a small, free museum inside which is open to the public from 9am to 4:15pm Monday to Friday. Tours are offered on Saturdays at 10am and 2pm. These tours are extremely popular and should be booked as far in advance as possible. There is a charge.

Exit the Bell Foundry and bear left along Whitechapel Road. Having crossed Adler Street, you'll pass an open park. This was the site of:

7. **St. Mary's Church,** a 13th-century structure destroyed by bombs during World War II. St. Mary's was the "White Chapel" that imparted its name to the entire

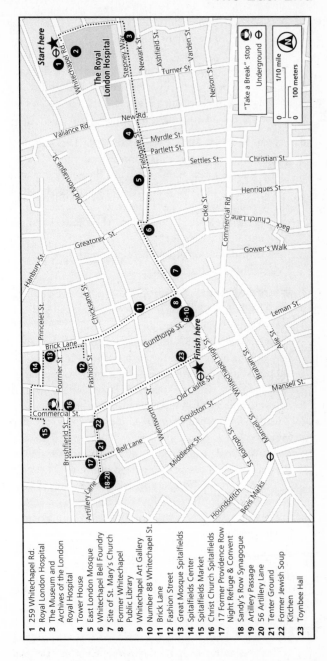

area—it was common in the 13th century to lime-wash the exteriors of important buildings.

Keep going along Whitechapel Road, and cross Whitechapel Road via the traffic lights outside the gates of the park. Bear left over Osborn Street, on the other side of which the road becomes Whitechapel High Street. Half a block ahead on your right is the:

8. Former **Whitechapel Public Library.** This was once the hub of London's Jewish intellectual community, a group that included humanist Jacob Bronowsky, mathematician Selig Brodetsky, poet Isaac Rosenberg, and novelist Israel Zangwill. These men and others met almost daily in the reference reading room, where they exchanged ideas and debated intensely.

A few doors along on the right, past Aldgate East Underground Station, is the:

9. **Whitechapel Art Gallery,** 80 Whitechapel High St. (© 020/7522-7888). Built between 1897 and 1899, this unusual Art Nouveau building was designed by C. H. Townsend. Founded by Canon Samuel Barnet, the gallery here originally displayed the works of local Impressionist painter Mark Gertler. A lively lecture series attracted such luminaries as George Bernard Shaw. Today, highly renowned pieces of modern art are often exhibited here. The gallery is open Tuesday through Wednesday and Friday through Sunday 11am to 6pm, and Thursday 11am to 9pm. Admission is free to most exhibits, although there is one paying exhibit per year.

Continue along Whitechapel High Street. Immediately before Gunthorpe Street, pause to look up at and admire the intricate badge of Jewish symbols set within a Star of David above:

10. **Number 88 Whitechapel High Street.** The elaborate badge is the work of Polish Jewish artist Arthur Szyk. The ornamentation formerly adorned the offices of the *Jewish Daily Post*, England's first (albeit short-lived) Anglo-Jewish daily newspaper, founded in 1935 by H. P. Sanders.

Turn right through the arch into Gunthorpe Street (passing the apartment block on the left that has the year

1888 above it and which was formerly Sir George's Home For Girls). Walk the length of Gunthorpe Street, turn right along Wentworth Street, and then turn left along:

11. **Brick Lane,** so-named because bricks and tiles were manufactured here in the 16th century. Today, this is one of the area's busiest trading streets. Once home to the Jewish community, it has accommodated many immigrants over the centuries, and is now home to a thriving Asian population. The leather trade is an important part of Brick Lane's economy, and the street is lined with an impressive variety of Indian and Bangladeshi curry houses.

Continue along Brick Lane until you arrive on the left at:

12. **Fashion Street.** This street has been home to several well-known writers, including playwright Arnold Wesker and Hollywood screenwriter Wolf Mankowitz. Another resident was Israel Zangwill, whose first novel, *Children of the Ghetto,* was published in 1892, while he was teaching at a local Jewish school. Zangwill's phonetic translations of Yiddish East End speech angered the school authorities, who were trying to teach correct English, and he was required to resign from his teaching position. Zangwill later became the first secretary of the World Zionist Federation.

Writer Jack London's reputation was already established when he took up residence here in 1902. He had come to England for the coronation of Edward VII and was dismayed to observe the contrast between the opulence of the event and the dire poverty of so many Londoners. Wanting to experience firsthand the hardships of the impoverished, he decided to live in the East End. He recorded his experiences in *The People of the Abyss.*

Backtrack to Brick Lane, go left, and keep walking along Brick Lane until you arrive at its junction with Fournier Street. On the opposite side is the:

13. **Great Mosque Spitalfields.** This building, more than any other in the neighborhood, reflects the area's changing demographics. Built in 1743 as a Huguenot School and chapel, it was acquired 50 years later by the London

Society, a group dedicated to converting Jews to Christianity. It offered £50 to any convert who agreed to resettle in a Christian district. By 1892, however, when it issued its final report, the society acknowledged that it had made only 16 bona fide converts. The building then became a Methodist chapel, was later converted into the Great Synagogue Spitalfields, and in 1976 was sold to the Bangladeshi community, which converted it to a mosque.

Turn left into Fournier Street, where the houses were built specifically for the Huguenot refugees who fled France after the revocation of the Edict of Nantes in 1685. Because many of the refugees were skillful weavers, the houses were designed with large attic windows to provide as much daylight as possible for the refugees to work at their looms. Many of the houses have now been beautifully restored.

Three quarters of the way along Fournier Street, go right along Wilkes Street, and take the first right into Princelet Street. Again, several of the houses along this street have been lovingly restored, and the street as a whole is blessed with the ambience of a bygone age. Keep to the left side of the street and pause outside:

14. **Spitalfields Center,** 19 Princelet St. (✆ 020/7247-5352; www.19Princeletstreet.org.uk). As with most of the buildings on the street, this house, dating from 1719, was built for the Huguenot silk merchants (note the weaver's bobbin hanging from the outside of the building). In 1870, the United Friends Synagogue was constructed in the former garden area. The synagogue remained active until 1980, and much of the interior survives, from the candelabra still suspended from the ceiling, to the panels in the ladies' galleries inscribed with the names of the congregation members who contributed to the synagogue's upkeep. The building has the distinctions of being the oldest purpose-built "minor synagogue" in the East End and the third-oldest synagogue in England. Although it is rarely open to the public, plans are afoot to turn the building into a museum of immigrant life.

In 1969, David Rodinsky, a reclusive Jewish scholar who lived in an attic room above the synagogue, disappeared. He remained largely forgotten until his room was rediscovered in 1980 by workmen who, it is said, tripped over a mummified cat as they entered what proved to be a veritable time capsule. Writings, annotated books, maps, gramophone records, and clothes lay scattered about the room. The dust-coated contents had apparently lain undisturbed since their owner's departure. The story of Rodinsky's mysterious disappearance, and the subsequent mythology that came to surround him, inspired Rachel Lichtenstein and Iain Sinclair's evocative book, *Rodinsky's Room.*

Go back to Wilkes Street, turn left, and take the first right through Puma Court. On arrival at Commercial Street, pause to look over at:

15. **Spitalfields Market.** This market flourished following the devastation caused to the nearby City of London by the Great Fire of 1666. By the 19th century, it had become London's leading market for fruit and vegetables. The building you are about to enter dates from 1887. In the 1980s, the fruit and vegetable market moved out. The lofty structure is now occupied by a veritable cornucopia of craft stalls, second-hand book stalls, and record stalls, plus food shops that serve a diverse and mouth-watering range of ethnic foods. The market is at its liveliest and busiest on Sunday mornings.

Go left along Commercial Street and at the junction with Fournier Street:

Take a Break **The Ten Bells.** Built in the mid– 19th century, this East End watering hole was formerly known as the Jack the Ripper, in commemoration of the 1888 murders that took place in the streets hereabouts. It reverted to its Victorian name in 1988. Its interior boasts exquisite 19th century tiling that includes a colorful tiled wall panel depicting "Spitalfields in ye olden times."

Exit the Ten Bells and cross over Fournier Street to pause outside:

16. **Christ Church Spitalfields** (**℅ 020/7247-7202**), built between 1714 and 1729. The masterpiece of architect Nicholas Hawksmoor, this building originally served Huguenot refugees.

Continue along Commercial Street and cross it via the pedestrian crossing. Go straight along Whites Row, passing the Whites Row Car Park that lines the right side of the street. Turn right onto Crispin Street. On the left is the former:

17. **Providence Row Night Refuge and Convent,** built in 1868 and run by the order of the Sisters of Mercy. During the late 19th century, the order provided lodging "to the destitute from all parts, without distinction of creed, colour, and country." At the time of writing, the building is being converted to upscale apartments.

Continue along Crispin Street and turn left onto Brushfield Street. If you are doing the walk on a cold winter's day, or if you are simply in the mood for some good old-fashioned English comfort food, then a few doors along on the left:

Take a Break **The Sausage and Mash Cafe** occupies one of the area's 18th-century buildings, and offers a menu of up to 20 different types of sausage served with mashed potatoes and onion gravy. Vegetarian options are also available.

Continue along Brushfield Street, then go left into Gun Street, and right along Artillery Lane. Follow Artillery Lane as it bends left, then turn left into Sandy's Row. A little way along, on the left, is the:

18. **Sandy's Row Synagogue,** 4A Sandy's Row (© 020/ 7253-8311). This building was originally a Huguenot church. In 1867, it was leased to Dutch Jews, who used it for their Society of Kindness and Truth. You can view it by appointment.

Continue on Sandy's Row and then go left along:

19. **Artillery Passage.** This narrow and atmospheric passage is lined with Victorian, or at least Victorian-looking, shops, most of which possess 19th-century facades. In the 16th century, this area comprised open fields outside the city walls and was used primarily for recreational purposes. In 1537, Henry VIII granted a Royal Warrant to the Honorable Artillery Company and later permitted it to practice in these fields. Several streets in this area bear the

name Artillery, derived from the Artillery barracks that once stood here.

Continue through Artillery Passage until you reach Artillery Lane. Two doors along, on the right, you will find:

20. **56 Artillery Lane.** This building dates from 1756 and is widely considered to be the finest Georgian storefront in London. Its first occupant was a silk merchant by the name of Francis Rybot.

    Walk the short distance to the end of Artillery Lane, cross over Bell Lane, and continue back into White's Row. Take the first right onto:

21. **Tenter Ground.** Until the 1820s, this was a wide-open space used for drying fabric; the cloth was attached to large hooks and then stretched over wooden frames. From this practice came the expression "to be on tenterhooks."

    At the end of Tenter Ground, turn left into Brune Street. Walk 1 block to the former:

22. **Jewish Soup Kitchen,** 9 Brune Street. Opened in 1902 (actually the year 5662 in the Jewish calendar), primarily to feed the area's Jewish poor, this kosher kitchen was busiest during the Great Depression, when it provided meals to more than 5,000 people each week. Although it is no longer open to the public—or, for that matter, serving meals—the building's impressive frontage can still be admired.

    At the end of Brune Street, turn right into Toynbee Street. At the end of Toynbee Street, go left along Wentworth Street, then turn right onto Commercial Street. Cross over the pedestrian crossing, bear right, and continue to walk past the length of long, red-brick wall. After you've passed the wall, go left through the gates to:

23. **Toynbee Hall.** These 1880s buildings give the impression of an English Manor house, and seem strangely at odds with the immediate surroundings. The hall is named for Arnold Toynbee—the young Oxford historian who proposed the idea that undergraduates from both Oxford and Cambridge should spend time among less fortunate members of society and impart their learning to them.

Toynbee died in 1883, and his friend, the Reverend Samuel Barnett, vicar of St. Jude's church on Commercial Street, opened Toynbee Hall a year later. Here, middle-class academics endeavored to take the benefits of culture and education into some of the most sordid and crime-ridden enclaves of the Victorian metropolis. The hall flourished for 15 years, but in 1900 Barnett was forced to admit that his ideals and ambitions had not been universally adopted in the area. Today, the buildings provide accommodation for overseas students and senior citizens.

Backtrack to Commercial Street, turn left, walk to the traffic lights, and cross to Aldgate East Underground Station, where the tour ends.

Clerkenwell

Start: Barbican Underground Station.

Finish: Farringdon Underground Station.

Time: 2 hours.

Best Time: Weekends, when less traffic permits a more pleasant stroll.

Worst Time: None.

London's "hidden village," Clerkenwell is a quirky little quarter, nestled between Bloomsbury and the City of London. Its heyday came in the 17th century, when upper-class people built stately homes near the water well for which this area was named. Whether we realize it or not, many of us know the Clerkenwell of the 19th century through Charles Dickens—many of the sights, smells, and sounds described in his novels undoubtedly came from these streets. During those years, the area was highly industrialized, densely populated, and tragically poor. It has since been revitalized, though many of the Georgian and Victorian buildings still hint at Clerkenwell's colorful history.

• • • • • • • • • • • • • •

Exit Barbican Underground Station and turn left onto Aldersgate Street. Take the first left into Carthusian Street and walk 1 block, on the right, to:

1. **Charterhouse Square,** a 14th-century burial pit located just on the other side of this fence. A number of catastrophes have befallen London over the years, but few have been as devastating as the bubonic plague—Black Death—that killed thousands in 1348. Churchyards, the traditional burial grounds of the time, couldn't cope with the overwhelming number of deaths, so plague pits for mass burials were dug in several open spaces around London. This pit, which originally covered 5.3 hectares (13 acres), was donated to the city in 1350 by Sir Walter de Manny, a knight who sympathized with victims of the Black Death. Although chronicler John Stow later claimed that 50,000 people were buried here, most historians don't believe that London's entire population at the time exceeded 35,000.

With the fence on your left, continue through Charterhouse Square until you see:

2. **Florin Court,** the Art Deco building on your right. If you're a fan of the Poirot TV series, starring David Suchet, you might recognize this building. Its facade was used for the external shots of the apartment of Agatha Christie's clever Belgian detective, he of the "little gray cells."

Follow the fence around, and then turn right through the huge wooden doors of the:

3. **Charterhouse** (✆ 020/7253-9503), founded by Sir Walter de Manny in 1370 as a monastery for Carthusian monks. Built by Henry Yevele, Edward III's master mason, the house enabled the monks to live in solitude 6 days a week. On Sundays, they came together in the refectory for their meal and then were allowed a 3-hour outdoor recess—the only time they were permitted to talk to one another.

In 1535, the monastery's prior, John Houghton, invited Thomas Cromwell, then Henry VIII's vicar general, to a discussion about the king's supremacy as head of the English church. Cromwell responded by arranging for the monks to be imprisoned and tried for "treacherously

Clerkenwell

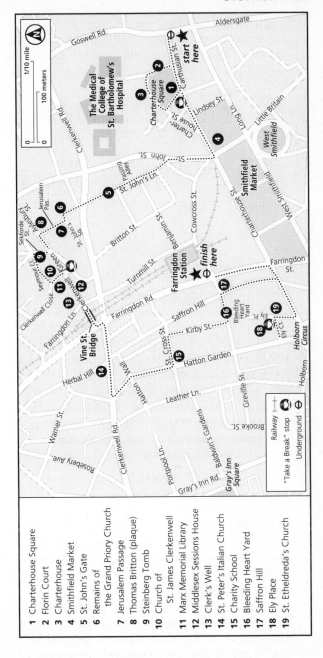

1. Charterhouse Square
2. Florin Court
3. Charterhouse
4. Smithfield Market
5. St. John's Gate
6. Remains of
   the Grand Priory Church
7. Jerusalem Passage
8. Thomas Britton (plaque)
9. Steinberg Tomb
10. Church of
    St. James Clerkenwell
11. Marx Memorial Library
12. Middlesex Sessions House
13. Clerk's Well
14. St. Peter's Italian Church
15. Charity School
16. Bleeding Heart Yard
17. Saffron Hill
18. Ely Place
19. St. Etheldreda's Church

machinating and desiring to deprive the King of his title as supreme head of the church." After his conviction, Houghton was hung, drawn, and quartered. As a warning to others, one of his arms was nailed onto the monastery's entrance gate.

The monastery surrendered to the king in 1537, and eventually came into the possession of John Dudley, Duke of Northumberland. It is possible that Dudley used the Charterhouse as a residence for his son, Guilford Dudley, and Guilford's wife, Lady Jane Grey. In July 1553, upon the death of Edward VI, Grey was proclaimed queen. Afraid that Edward's Roman Catholic sister, Mary, would turn Protestant England Catholic if she became queen, John Dudley persuaded the young king to name Jane his successor. However, she was queen for only 9 days: Once Mary's claim to the throne was recognized, Jane and her husband were tried for high treason and then beheaded. This story might sound familiar if you've seen the movie *Lady Jane,* starring Helena Bonham Carter and Cary Elwes.

The Charterhouse was purchased in 1611 (for £13,000, a handsome sum at the time) by Thomas Sutton, who turned the building into a school for poor boys and a retirement home for men. Until 1892, the school successfully educated thousands of disadvantaged Londoners, including Baron Baden-Powell, founder of the Scouts movement; author William Makepeace Thackeray; and John Wesley, founder of the Methodist Church.

Guided tours leave from the main gate Wednesdays at 2:15pm from April to July.

Exit the Charterhouse, turn right, and continue through the iron gates to Charterhouse Street. On the right is the:

☕ Take a Break **Fox and Anchor Public House,** 116 Charterhouse St. Known locally as an "early house," this tavern is specially licensed to serve alcohol between 6:30 and 9:30am, enabling it to accommodate the early morning workers at Smithfield Market, London's primary meat market. If you're taking this tour early in the day, stop here for one of the pub's famous English breakfasts.

Exit the pub, turn right along Charterhouse Street, and continue for half a block. The large building you'll see on the opposite side of the street is:

4. **Smithfield Market,** formerly the "smoothfield," a grassy area just outside the city gates where a weekly horse fair was held during the Middle Ages. In 1638, the City Corporation established a cattle market here. As the city expanded, encircling the market, residents complained about the general filth and the drunken behavior of market workers. So, in 1855 the livestock market was moved to Islington. The current market building dates from the 1860s and was designed by Sir Horace Jones, whose later works include Tower Bridge.

With the market on your left, continue 1 block down Charterhouse Street and turn right onto St. John Street. Cross at the pedestrian crossing, bear right, and then fork left into St. John's Lane. Continue until you arrive at:

5. **St. John's Gate,** St. John's Lane (*©* **020/7324-4070**). Once the main entrance to the 12th-century Priory of the Knights Hospitallers of St. John of Jerusalem, this is the only monastic gatehouse left in London. The priory no longer exists, but the gateway, dating from 1504, has served a variety of functions.

During the reign of Henry VIII (1509–47), the gatehouse was used as office space for the king's administrators. From 1731 to 1781, it was the headquarters of *Gentleman's Magazine,* a popular periodical whose contributors included Oliver Goldsmith and Samuel Johnson. (Johnson was given a special room in which to write; it's said that he literally locked himself away so that no one could get in and tempt him out or disturb him.)

In subsequent years, the gatehouse was turned into the parish watch house; later it became the Old Jerusalem Tavern. In 1874, it was turned into the property of the Most Venerable Order of the Hospital of St. John of Jerusalem, a Protestant order founded in 1831 to uphold the traditions of the medieval Hospitallers. It was here that the St. John's Ambulance Brigade, one of the world's first, was founded in 1877.

Today the gatehouse serves as a museum and library, and it is open Monday to Friday from 10am to 5pm and Saturday from 10am to 4pm. Tours are offered on Tuesday, Friday, and Saturday at 11am and 2:30pm. There's an admission charge.

Walk through the gate and continue straight ahead, across busy Clerkenwell Road. Proceed into St. John's Square. The iron gates on your right guard the:

6. **Remains of the Grand Priory Church,** the 12th-century church for which the gatehouse was the main entrance. All the monastic foundations that flourished in medieval times were secularized by Henry VIII in 1540, leaving few traces behind. The remains of the church, situated beyond the gates, are some of the best-preserved examples of those monasteries.

With your back to the church gates, bear right into:

7. **Jerusalem Passage,** a small thoroughfare that was once the site of the priory's northern gate. Most of the structures you see here today were erected on medieval foundations.

At the end of the short passage, high up on your right, is a green wall plaque commemorating:

8. **Thomas Britton** (1644–1714), a local coal merchant and lover of music. Knowledgeable in chemistry, a respected collector of rare books, and a talented musician, Britton was widely known as the "Musical Coalman." A sort of Renaissance man, he established an informal music club that met above his rather dingy shop, formerly located on this site. The club attracted celebrated musicians of the day as well as members of the royal court.

Turn left onto Aylesbury Street, then take the first right onto Sekforde Street. Stay to the left and follow the road left into St. James's Walk. Turn left through the iron gates into the churchyard of St. James's, Clerkenwell. By the steps you will find:

9. **Steinberg Tomb,** the grave of a murdered family. The Steinberg murders horrified the country when they occurred in 1834. Although the stone's inscription has worn away, you can still make out the name Steinberg—the surname of Ellen and her four young children, who

were stabbed to death on September 8 by their husband and father, John Nicholas Steinberg, before he turned the knife on himself. Londoners were so distressed by the murders that they took up a collection to have Ellen and her children interred here.

Because the murderer committed suicide, he couldn't be buried in a churchyard. Outraged citizens took Steinberg's coffin to a pauper's graveyard on nearby Ray Street. The burial took place at night; tipped from the coffin directly into the grave, the corpse was struck over the head with an iron mallet and a stake was driven through his heart.

Proceed counterclockwise around the church and exit via the iron gates to turn left onto Clerkenwell Close. A little way along on the left is the:

10. **Church of St. James Clerkenwell,** Clerkenwell Gardens. Once part of a Benedictine nunnery dedicated to St. Mary, this church survived Henry VIII's dissolution in 1539. It was rebuilt in 1625, and Samuel Pepys, the diarist, records attending the services to ogle the local beauties! Rebuilt again between 1778 and 1782, the church authorities appear to have still been worried by the temptation afforded to any latter-day Pepys. The steep staircases and fitted "modesty boards" (iron screens running from ankle to knee length around the banisters) were intended to prevent the gentlemen of the parish from looking up the ladies' skirts as they ascended to the balcony.

Exit onto Clerkenwell Close and proceed ahead onto Clerkenwell Green; on the corner you'll find the:

Take a Break **Crown Tavern,** 43 Clerkenwell Green. Established in 1641 and rebuilt in 1815, the Crown gained fame in the 19th century because of its Apollo Concert Room, a live-music hall that was open every evening. The downstairs room of this bilevel pub still displays Victorian-era playbills. Today, the only entertainment is conversation among the patrons.

In the main bar, you can still open and close the "snob screens"—screens that were placed here long ago to separate those who belonged to the working class from those of the middle class (who were in a private bar). A good selection of food and drink is always available.

Exit the tavern and cross Clerkenwell Close; three doors down, on the right, is the:

11. **Marx Memorial Library,** 37A Clerkenwell Green (© 020/7253-1485). Though this building dates from 1738, it acquired its present designation in 1933—the 50th anniversary of Karl Marx's death. The library is dedicated to Marxism, Socialism, and the history of labor movements. Inside, you can see the Lenin room (where he edited *Iskra* in 1902 and 1903) and browse more than 100,000 books and periodicals. The library is open Monday to Thursday afternoons from 1pm to 6pm.

Continue along Clerkenwell Green. The large building opposite is the:

12. **Middlesex Sessions House,** a former courthouse built in 1779 by architect John Rogers. The stone relief adorning the front facade represents Justice and Mercy. By 1919, London's expanding criminal population had outgrown this building, and when the courts moved, the house was converted into offices. In 1979, the building was acquired by the Masonic Foundation and restored to its former glory.

Continue walking along the right side of Clerkenwell Green. At the end, turn right into Farringdon Lane. A few doors down on the right is the:

13. **Clerk's Well,** 16 Farringdon Lane, the water supply that gives this area its name. It was around the original well, mentioned as early as 1174, that the parish clerks of London gathered to perform medieval miracle plays. This activity led people to call the well *Fons Clericorum* ("Clerk's Well"), a name that was subsequently passed on to the area.

Backtrack along Farringdon Lane and take the first right into Vine Street Bridge. Cross over Farringdon Road at the traffic lights, and proceed ahead into Clerkenwell Road. Continue across Herbal Hill; a few doors down on the right is:

14. **St. Peter's Italian Church,** designed by J. M. Brydon and opened in 1863 to serve the large Italian population of the vicinity (the area was known at the time as Little Italy). The church has a strong musical tradition, and in the 19th and early 20th centuries, Italian opera singers including Enrico Caruso often sang at mass here.

    Exit the church and cautiously cross Clerkenwell Road, bearing right and then taking the first left into Hatton Garden, which has been the center of London's jewelry trade since 1836. Two blocks down, at the corner of St. Cross Street, is the former:

15. **Charity School,** designed by Sir Christopher Wren. This building was originally a small chapel intended to serve the spiritual needs of the neighborhood; later, it became a charity school. Above the door are figures depicting the students of the time. The girl on the right holds in one hand a parchment, on which is written the cost of her expenses, while her other hand is outstretched to encourage passersby to make a contribution. The building is now used for offices.

    Continue along St. Cross Street and make the first right into Kirby Street. At its end, turn left into Greville Street. The first turn on your right is:

16. **Bleeding Heart Yard.** In 1576, early in her reign, Elizabeth I decided to deed this land to her friend Sir Christopher Hatton. The only problem was that she didn't own the land; it belonged to the Bishop of Ely. When the queen asked him to relinquish it, he refused, prompting the queen to write: "Proud Prelate, remember what thou werst before we made thee. Comply, or by God we shall defrock thee." And so the bishop complied.

    Popular myth has it that Sir Christopher's wife, Lady Hatton, entered into a pact with the devil here. As the story goes, one evening, in the midst of a party, the devil appeared and took Lady Hatton away. According to the legend: " . . . *out in the courtyard, and just in that part where the pump stands—lay bleeding a large human heart.*" The pump is no longer here—nor, for that matter, is the heart—but the yard's name commemorates the sinister pact.

Exit right from Bleeding Heart Yard, continue 1 block along Greville Street, and then turn right into:

17. **Saffron Hill,** named for the spice that was once sold here. Saffron was popular in the days before refrigeration because of its ability to disguise the taste of rancid meat.

In the 18th century, this area was part of the gardens of the Bishop of Ely. By the 19th century, Saffron Hill had become a notorious criminal rookery. Theft was so common that it was said that one could have a handkerchief stolen at one end of the street and buy it back at the other. In *Oliver Twist,* Charles Dickens referred to Saffron Hill, calling it Field Court; this was the place where Fagin had his lair, and where young children were trained in the art of pickpocketing.

At the end of Saffron Hill, go up the steps and turn right. Half a block down, go through the gates into:

18. **Ely Place,** former site of the palace of the Bishops of Ely until Elizabeth I demanded that the land be given to Sir Christopher Hatton (see Stop 16, above). The nineteen charming houses that stand here comprise London's most perfectly preserved Georgian precinct. Until the 1930s, Ely Place was controlled by the Council of Cambridgeshire, not London. Consequently, the Metropolitan Police had no jurisdiction here and couldn't enter or arrest any suspect who walked through the gates on your right. As you enter the gates, you pass the beadle's hut, with its white chimney.

Farther inside the courtyard, hidden away on your left, is:

19. **St. Etheldreda's Church,** Ely Place. Built at the end of the 13th century, the church was named for St. Etheldreda (St. Awdry), an abbess who died in A.D. 679 from a throat tumor that was said to have been inflicted on her as punishment for her fondness for beaded necklaces. The type of devotional beads she wore (which actually were of cheap quality) came to be known as St. Awdrys, which was shortened to tawdry—a word still in use today.

Enter the church, which is best known for its ancient crypt and spectacular postwar stained glass. The arches of the crypt, dating from 1251, combine Norman and Gothic styles of architecture.

Exit the church and return to Ely Place. Turn right at Ely Court. On your right you'll arrive at:

☕ **Take a Break** **Ye Olde Mitre Tavern,** 1 Ely Court (✆ **020/7405-4751**). Built in 1546 for the servants of the Bishop of Ely, this beautiful Elizabethan pub was known to Samuel Johnson, Charles Dickens, and other famous local wordsmiths. Before you enter, check out the cherry tree that's now preserved behind glass by the front door. This tree used to be the boundary marker between the land that the Bishop of Ely was allowed to keep and the land he was compelled to give Sir Christopher Hatton (in return for one red rose a year). The Mitre offers a good selection of real ales and is justifiably famous for its toasted sandwiches.

Exit the tavern, backtrack to Ely Place, and turn right. At Charterhouse Street, turn left and then turn left again onto Farringdon Road. One block along, turn right into Cowcross Street to arrive at Farringdon Underground Station.

Bloomsbury

Start: Holborn Underground Station.

Finish: Holborn Underground Station.

Time: 2 hours.

Best Time: Monday through Saturday 10am to 6pm, and Sunday afternoon.

Worst Time: Sunday morning.

Bloomsbury dates from the late 17th century. It was laid out around a series of squares and was promoted as London's newest social center. In the early 20th century, it gained fame as the residence of the "Bloomsbury Group," a circle of writers and thinkers that included Clive and Vanessa Bell, E. M. Forster, Lytton Strachey, Bertrand Russell, John Maynard Keynes, and Leonard and Virginia Woolf.

Bloomsbury's convenient location, just north of Soho and west of the City of London, has been a significant factor in its development. And its proximity to businesses, shops, and theaters has long made this area a desirable place to live. Several large hotels and dozens of smaller B&Bs testify to Bloomsbury's appeal to visitors as well.

Bloomsbury

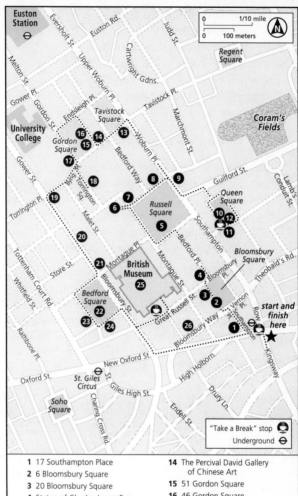

The class system is still quite evident in Bloomsbury—most of the land here is still owned by a single person, the Earl of Bedford. The two largest occupants, however, are the British Museum and the University of London, which keep the area alive with new faces and ideas. Bloomsbury has developed into an interesting, well-balanced mix of private residences and public institutions.

• • • • • • • • • • • • • • • • •

Exit Holborn Underground Station and cross High Holborn at the traffic light. Bear left, cross Southampton Row and, 1 block later, turn right into Southampton Place. This 18th-century street was named after the first Earl of Southampton. Several well-preserved Georgian houses from the 1740s line this block. On your left is:

1. **17 Southampton Place,** the former home of John Henry Cardinal Newman (1801–90). An eminent theologian, Newman became a leading member of the ill-fated Oxford movement, an attempt to return England's Protestant Anglican Church to its traditional heritage. He failed to persuade England's relatively progressive clergy that this approach was desirable, but his "Oxfords," named for the university where the movement was based, went so far back to their religious roots that Newman became a Roman Catholic.

Continue along Southampton Place; go over the pedestrian crossing to walk clockwise around Bloomsbury Square. The first house to your left on the square, just after the traffic lights, is:

2. **6 Bloomsbury Square,** the former home of Isaac D'Israeli (1766–1848), author and father of the Victorian-era Prime Minister Benjamin Disraeli (who changed the spelling of his surname). Isaac was born in England to Sephardic Jews who had fled from persecution in Spain. Educated in Amsterdam, he was both an intellectual and a respected writer. One of D'Israeli's literary works, *Curiosities of Literature* (1791), a volume of anecdotes and essays, went into 12 editions.

Continue around the square to look across the road at:

3. **20 Bloomsbury Square,** once home to Gertrude Stein (1874–1946) and her brother Leo. The Steins rented an apartment here in 1902, after Gertrude failed to get her medical degree at Johns Hopkins University in Baltimore. A voracious reader and writer, Gertrude enjoyed living near the British Museum's Reading Room, where she immersed herself in the works of novelist Anthony Trollope. But Stein complained about London's depressing grayness; after spending a year on Bloomsbury Square, she left for Paris, the city that would become her adopted home. There she lived with Alice B. Toklas.

   Keeping the gardens to your right, walk a few steps farther and pause at the:

4. **Statue of Charles James Fox,** 18th-century leader of the Whigs in the House of Commons. Plump and convivial, Fox (1749–1806) had an enormous appetite for both food and drink. His charisma and oratorical talent established him as England's leading radical. He opposed war with America and expressed sympathy for the French Revolution. George III profoundly distrusted him, but the Prince of Wales (later George IV) was his close friend. The statue depicts Fox as a champion of English freedom—a toga-clad Consul holding a copy of the Magna Carta, with the seal faithfully copied from the original in the British Museum.

   With your back to the statue, cross the road and go straight ahead into Bedford Place, a street that ends at:

5. **Russell Square.** Because of its proximity to museums, hotels, and the Underground Station, this square has become the de facto center of Bloomsbury. Constructed in 1800, it's named after the Russell family, which is headed by the Earl of Bedford, one of London's largest landowners. Because of its beauty and excellent location—close to both the City and the West End—Russell Square and the surrounding area have always been popular with lawyers, physicians, and other well-to-do professionals.

   In the gardens is a **statue of Francis Russell,** fifth Duke of Bedford (1765–1802), who oversaw the development of much of Bloomsbury on the former site of his family's ancestral home, Bedford House. Because the duke served on the first Board of Agriculture and helped develop modern methods of farming, the statue depicts him with one hand resting on a plow and the other holding a sheaf of corn.

Turn left onto the square and cross it via the pedestrian crossing, toward the gardens. Continue clockwise to cross the next two pedestrian crossings by the red phone boxes. Bear left and take the first right through the gates to the courtyard of:

6. **Senate House,** designed by Charles Holden and completed in 1937. Known locally as the "Big House in Bloomsbury," it's now the administration building of the University of London.

During World War II, the building housed the Ministry of Information, where journalists came for official news releases about the war. Graham Greene, who worked here, described it as "a beacon guiding the German planes toward King's Cross and St. Pancras Stations. . . . I wrote a letter to the *Spectator* with the title 'Bloomsbury Lighthouse' [after which] the lights were dimmed."

George Orwell used this building as a model for the Ministry of Truth in his novel *1984*. The building was called "Minitrue" in Newspeak, the official language of the totalitarian state portrayed in the novel. As Orwell described it, "The Ministry of Truth . . . was startlingly different from any other object in sight. It was an enormous pyramidical structure of glittering white concrete, soaring up, terrace after terrace, three hundred metres into the air. . . . It was too strong, it could not be stormed. A thousand rocket bombs would not batter it down."

Backtrack to the gates and turn left onto Russell Square. Continue walking clockwise around the square toward the white balcony of:

7. **24 Russell Square,** where poet T. S. Eliot worked as a book publisher with the firm Faber and Faber. (In addition to being a successful writer, Eliot was a prosperous businessman.) Eliot was quite generous with his wealth, assisting his less well-to-do friends; in a diary, fellow writer Roy Campbell (1902–57) related that when he and

Dylan Thomas were in need of money, they called on "his grace" (Eliot) and were rewarded lavishly.

Continue clockwise around Russell Square to:

8. **21 Russell Square,** the former home of Sir Samuel Romilly (1757–1818). A lawyer and legal reformer, Romilly is best remembered for his success in reducing England's large number of offenses that were punishable by death. In addition, along with his friend and confidant abolitionist William Wilberforce, Romilly played a significant role in stopping Britain's slave trade in the Caribbean and elsewhere.

Continue; go over the crossing and then pause at the junction with Woburn Place to admire the:

9. **Hotel Russell,** perhaps the most beautiful building in Bloomsbury. The hotel opened in 1900, and its ornate facade is one of the finest examples of late Victorian Renaissance architecture in London. Prospective guests might want to know that, alas, the interior (consisting of some 300 rooms) isn't as elegant. Still, it's worth a look.

The Russell is on the site of the former Pankhurst home. England's most famous suffragettes, Emmeline Pankhurst and her daughters, Christabel and Sylvia, lived here from 1888 to 1893; during the first decade of the 20th century, the Pankhursts led the fight in England for women's right to vote and other forms of enfranchisement.

Cross to the Hotel Russell and continue along Russell Square, turning left after the hotel onto Guilford Street. Take your second right down a narrow passageway, Queen Anne's Walk, to enter:

10. **Queen Square,** a pretty plaza that was laid out in the early 18th century and named after Queen Anne. Once a fancy residential square, the green is now surrounded by hospitals and is a popular lunching spot for local workers.

Walk counterclockwise around the square to arrive at:

Take a Break **Queen's Larder.** This comfortable tavern serves good food and drink but deserves special mention for its unusual history. When George III became mentally ill, he took up residence nearby, at the home of his attending physician, Dr. Willis. In order to help her husband, Queen Charlotte rented cellar space beneath this building to store some of her husband's favorite foods. This pub, Queen's Larder (which means "pantry"), opened later in George III's reign.

Directly across the street from the pub is the:

11. **Church of St. George the Martyr** (1706), sometimes referred to as the "sweeps church." In the 18th and 19th centuries, poor boys—usually about 8 to 10 years old— often worked at cleaning chimneys, using their small bodies as brushes. Sympathizing with the plight of these impoverished youngsters, a local resident, Capt. James South, established a charity at this church to help them.

Cross the street to the square's inside sidewalk and continue walking counterclockwise around the square. On the south side of the square, pause at the:

12. **Water Pump.** This iron pump, dating from the early 1900s, commemorates the fact that Queen Square was once a water reservoir for the surrounding community. Times have changed, however, and the pump now carries a warning: UNFIT FOR DRINKING.

Continue around the square, step inside the gardens if you wish, and then backtrack to the Russell Hotel. With the hotel on your right, walk 2 long blocks up Woburn Place to Tavistock Square. Turn left on Tavistock Square and stop outside the:

13. **Tavistock Hotel,** a large, ugly building that occupies the site of Leonard and Virginia Woolf's former home. The Woolfs moved here in March 1929 and remained in Bloomsbury for 15 years. Virginia wrote in a large upstairs room that was illuminated by a skylight. The building's basement housed Hogarth Press, a publishing house that issued books by Woolf and T. S. Eliot, as well as English translations of the works of Sigmund Freud. Virginia left this house just 19 months before she drowned herself in the River Ouse.

Continue along Tavistock Square, cross Bedford Way, and continue into Gordon Square. A little way along, on the right, is:

14. **The Percival David Gallery of Chinese Art,** 53 Gordon Square (© **020/7387-3909**). This gallery houses the world's finest collection of Chinese ceramics outside China, encompassing approximately 1,700 items that reflect Chinese court taste from the 10th to the 18th centuries. The gallery is open Monday to Friday from 10:30am to 5pm; admission is free.

Exit the gallery, go right, and immediately turn right again to arrive at:

15. **51 Gordon Square,** the former home of Lytton Strachey (1880–1932). Strachey, a seminal writer and thinker, was an antiwar activist and conscientious objector during World War I. His well-regarded book *Eminent Victorians* is widely viewed as the first biographical novel—a new literary genre that mixed fact and fiction. When Strachey bought this house in 1919, he wrote to Virginia Woolf, "Very soon I foresee that the whole Square will become a sort of college, and *rencontres* in the garden I shudder to think of."

Next door, a plaque on the wall of no. 50 commemorates the **Bloomsbury Group,** London's famous 20th-century circle of writers, artists, and musicians. Singing, dancing, reading, debating, and a fair amount of debauchery brought publicity to the group's regular soirées. But not everyone was impressed by the events and antics of the Bloomsbury Group. Gertrude Stein dismissed them contemptuously as the "Young Men's Christian Association—with Christ left out."

Continue along for four doors to arrive at:

16. **46 Gordon Square,** the former home of John Maynard Keynes (1883–1946). An eminent economist, Keynes played a leading role in negotiations that led to the establishment of the International Monetary Fund. One of the world's most significant economic bodies, the International Monetary Fund is an organization of 184 countries working to foster global monetary cooperation, secure financial stability, facilitate international trade, promote high employment and sustainable economic growth, and reduce poverty.

Keynes turned his home into a meeting place for Bloomsbury's creative community, and gatherings here were often attended by Virginia Woolf and Lytton Strachey.

With your back to no. 46, cross over and enter the gardens (open Monday to Friday from 8am to 8pm). If they're locked, walk around to the opposite side. Once through the gardens, cross the road and turn left. One half block ahead, on Gordon Square (on the right), is the:

17. **Church of Christ the King,** designed by Raphael Brandon in 1853 and widely considered the finest mid-Victorian church in London. Now used by the University of London, it was originally a Catholic Apostolic Church. Enter the church to enjoy the exquisite stained-glass windows.

Exit the church and turn right. Cross Byng Place and proceed ahead to pass through the barrier into Torrington Square. A short way down, on the left, is:

18. **30 Torrington Square,** the former home of poet Christina Georgina Rossetti (1830–94), whose most famous narrative poem, "Goblin Market," was published in 1861. Though the publishing of this poem brought her fame, Rossetti was too shy to participate in the literary social gatherings of her day. Rossetti came from a literary family: She was significantly influenced by her brother, pre-Raphaelite poet and painter Dante Gabriel Rossetti.

Together with her mother, Christina moved to this house in 1876 to care for two elderly aunts. She never married. After the death of her mother, aunts, and brother, she published no more poetry, though the verses she wrote during those years were published after her death (1894). Today, her best known lyric is probably the Christmas carol "In the Bleak Midwinter."

Backtrack to Byng Place and turn left. Cross Malet Street to:

19. **Waterstone's Bookstore,** 82 Gower St. (© 020/ 7636-1577), formerly Dillon's. Founded in 1937 by Una Dillon, who had no previous book-selling experience, the shop soon expanded to become the official bookshop of

the University of London. Eccentric poet Dame Edith Sitwell (1887–1964) was a regular patron, often giving impromptu readings to astonished customers. If it's not mobbed with students, the store is definitely worth a browse.

Exit the bookstore and turn left into Gower Street. About a dozen B&Bs line the right side of this street. Most of the buildings on the left side are affiliated with the University of London. About 2 blocks down, on the left, is:

20. **Bonham Carter House,** 52 Gower St., standing on the site of a house and operating room where, on December 19, 1846, the first general anesthetic was administered in England.

Continue along Gower Street, crossing over Keppel Street to:

21. **2 Gower St.,** the former home of Dame Millicent Garrett Fawcett (1847–1929), one of England's most influential figures in the campaign for women's suffrage. Steadfastly opposed to aggressive tactics, Fawcett quietly rose to become the leader of the more moderate wing of the suffrage movement.

Immediately cross Gower Street and enter:

22. **Bedford Square,** Bloomsbury's last remaining wholly Georgian square. Laid out in 1775, the streets around the square were originally privately owned, and access was limited to residents and to those who had a legitimate reason to be in the area. Many of the square's pretty doorframes are made of Coade Stone, an artificial material known for its weather resistance. When the Coade Artificial Stone Manufactory was closed in 1840, the secret of the stone's composition was lost.

Walk counterclockwise around the square and pause outside:

23. **35 Bedford Square,** the former home of Thomas Wakley (1795–1862), a surgeon and friend of Charles Dickens who founded *The Lancet,* England's most prestigious medical journal. Wakley started the periodical in

order to criticize medical malpractice and nepotism, an endeavor that involved him in numerous libel actions. While serving as coroner for the West Middlesex Hospital, Wakley often allowed Dickens to attend his examinations—providing Dickens with plenty of fodder for his novels.

As you continue walking around the square, take note of the house at:

24. **42 Bedford Square.** From 1903 to 1917, this was the home of writer Sir Anthony Hope Hawkins (1863–1933), who is probably best known for his novel *The Prisoner of Zenda.*

Continue around Bedford Square, turn right onto Bloomsbury Street, and then take the first left onto Great Russell Street. Continue until you arrive at the:

25. **British Museum** (© **020/7636-1555**). With its unmatched collection of important finds from Egypt, Greece, Rome, Cyprus, Asia, and the Middle East, the British Museum merits its own full-day walking tour. The **Rosetta Stone,** whose discovery in the 19th century enabled modern scholars to understand Egyptian hieroglyphics, is at the entrance to the Egyptian sculpture gallery. The **Parthenon Sculptures,** formerly known as **The Elgin Marbles,** are the most famous objects in the museum's extensive collection of Greek antiquities; they were named for Lord Elgin, who took them from Athens. (The Greeks want them back and have mounted periodic campaigns exhorting the museum to return them.) Also on display are thousand-year-old pieces of Mesopotamian jewelry, Babylonian astronomical instruments, and Assyrian artifacts. Other fascinating exhibits display the contents of several Egyptian tombs, including wrapped mummies.

The museum's **Great Court,** resplendent in dazzling white marble, is truly breathtaking and leads to the absolutely stunning **Reading Room,** which has been restored to its 19th-century splendor and was opened to the public for the first time in its history in 2000. Dubbed by novelist George Gissing (1857–1902), "the valley of the Shadow of Books," the Reading Room was formerly open only to academics and specialist researchers and writers, who were obliged to obtain a so-called "reader's ticket." Now anyone can gasp in amazement at the soaring rows of books and stand beside reading desks at which the likes of Dickens, Marx, Shaw, George Eliot, and Rudyard Kipling (to name but a few) have sat and studied.

Just opposite the museum is the:

Take a Break **Museum Tavern,** 49 Great Russell St. Known as the "British Museum" until 1873, this pub's location across from the more famous British Museum guarantees a clientele that includes many museum visitors. In addition, the pub remains a popular refuge for local poets and scholars.

Leave the tavern and go left along Museum Street. Turn left onto Bloomsbury Way, where four doors down, on the left, is:

26. **St. George's Church,** Bloomsbury Way. Designed by Nicholas Hawksmoor, a pupil of Sir Christopher Wren, this church possesses one of London's most bizarre steeples, which Hawksmoor modeled on Pliny's description of the Mausoleum at Halicarnassus. Stepped like a pyramid, it is topped by a statue of George I posing as St. George in Roman dress. Horace Walpole contemptuously called it "a masterpiece of absurdity," while *A London Guide,* published in 1876, described it as "the most pretentious and ugliest edifice in the metropolis." Today the church is pleasant to visit, although its interior possesses an air of neglect.

Exit and turn left on Bloomsbury Way. Take the third right to Southampton Place, turn left, and follow New Oxford Street to Holborn Underground Station.

Soho

Start: Leicester Square Underground Station.

Finish: Piccadilly Circus Underground Station.

Time: 2½ hours, not counting cafe stops.

Best Times: Monday to Saturday from 9am to sunset.

Worst Times: Sunday, when most of Soho's shops are closed.

Since the 17th century, Soho has been London's most cosmopolitan area. Strolling around the locale, you can find traces of the Victorian era adjacent to theaters from the 1930s, beatnik cafes from the 1950s, rock hangouts from the 1960s, pornography shops from the 1970s, boutiques from the 1980s, and dance clubs from last night. After all these years, Soho is still the best place in London to find a great hidden restaurant or a fabulous all-night club. And though it's well known for its nightclubs, cinemas, theaters, and restaurants, Soho is also a complex amalgam of the successive immigrant groups that have established restaurants and other businesses here over the last 300 years. You'll find England's largest Chinatown here, as well as the heart of the country's film industry—Twentieth Century Fox and Warner Brothers have offices in the area.

This walk will give you an excellent overview of all that Soho has to offer. After you become acquainted with the area, return and explore those places that seem especially interesting.

● ● ● ● ● ● ● ● ● ● ● ● ● ● ● ● ●

Leave Leicester Square Underground Station via the Leicester Square exit and walk straight ahead to:

1. **Leicester Square,** Soho's most famous piazza. Leicester (*Les*-ter) Square was known as Lammas Fields until the 1630s, when it was inherited by the Earl of Leicester, who built his mansion here. The house became an alternative royal court in 1717, when the Prince of Wales (the future George II) took refuge here to escape the wrath of his tyrannical father, George I. Ironically, George II later became cruel to *his* son, Prince Frederick, who decided to move to Leicester House in 1742.

   When Leicester House was demolished in 1792, this area became rather dilapidated. There was a short-lived renaissance in 1851, when geographer James Wyld erected a model of the Earth in a dome-shaped building that filled the entire square. In 1874, a Member of Parliament, Albert Grant, purchased this land and commissioned James Knowles to design a public garden surrounding a memorial to Shakespeare and the busts of four famous residents: physicist Sir Isaac Newton, artists William Hogarth and Joshua Reynolds, and surgeon John Hunter. The London plane trees that now tower over the square were planted at this time. In 1975, Leicester Square was permanently closed to traffic, and in 1990, the Westminster County Council had the square renovated.

   At the center of Leicester Square is:

2. **Leicester Square Gardens.** This bucolic green is surrounded by an iron fence with a garden gate at each of the park's four corners. Each gate is named for a famous writer, artist, or scientist who lived in the immediate area, and each is marked with an appropriate statue.

   The entrance closest to you is **Hogarth Gate,** named for satirical artist/illustrator William Hogarth. Trained as an engraver and a painter, Hogarth became popular for

Soho

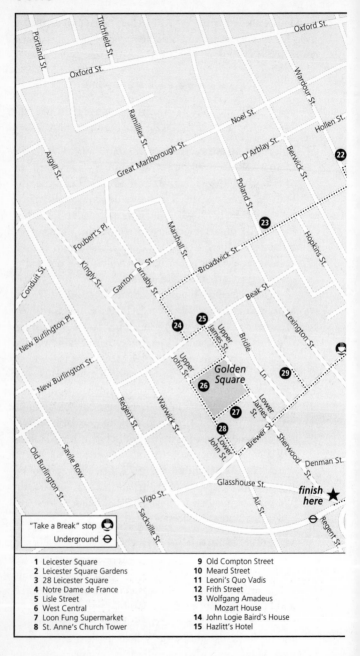

"Take a Break" stop 🐚
Underground ⊖

1 Leicester Square
2 Leicester Square Gardens
3 28 Leicester Square
4 Notre Dame de France
5 Lisle Street
6 West Central
7 Loon Fung Supermarket
8 St. Anne's Church Tower
9 Old Compton Street
10 Meard Street
11 Leoni's Quo Vadis
12 Frith Street
13 Wolfgang Amadeus
   Mozart House
14 John Logie Baird's House
15 Hazlitt's Hotel

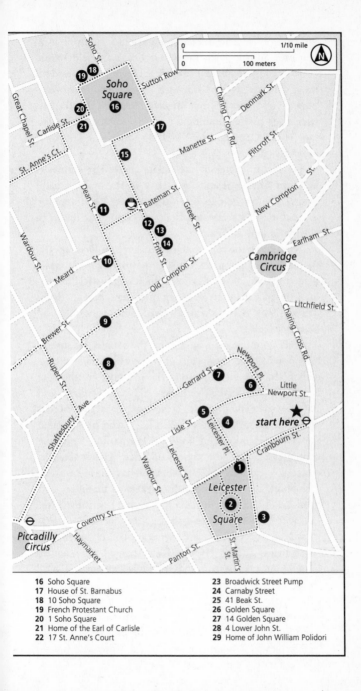

his biting portrayals of contemporary life. He lived at 30 Leicester Square (then known as Leicester Fields) from 1736 until his death in 1764. Here Hogarth produced his most famous works: *Marriage à la Mode, The Rake's Progress,* and *Industry and Idleness.* Hogarth's illustrations were often pirated, leading the artist to campaign for passage of the Copyright Law of 1735 (otherwise known as Hogarth's Act).

Go to the center of the square to see the **statue of William Shakespeare.** The scroll in the statue's hand reads: "There is no darkness but ignorance." Just opposite is a **statue of Charlie Chaplin,** consecrating the square to cinema as well as theater.

Walk along the path that leads away from Shakespeare. At the end of the path, you'll come to **Reynolds Gate,** named for Sir Joshua Reynolds, the celebrated 18th-century portrait painter and first president of the Royal Academy of Arts. Reynolds lived and painted at 47 Leicester Fields.

Walk counterclockwise around the square. Be sure to look down at the handprints of various film stars embedded in the pavement. Among the imprints are those of Ralph Fiennes, Sir Ian McKellen, Sylvester Stallone, and Billy Crystal. The next gate is **Newton Gate,** commemorating Sir Isaac Newton (1642–1727), who propounded the laws of motion and universal gravitation. Continue counterclockwise past the **Half-Price Ticket Booth,** where you can buy discounted same-day theater tickets. The booth is open at noon for tickets to matinees, and from 2:30 to 6:30pm for tickets to evening performances. Payment must be made in cash (traveler's checks and credit cards aren't accepted), and there's a small service charge.

The next gate is **Hunter Gate,** named for scientist John Hunter, a surgeon and anatomist who was a contemporary of Reynolds. Hunter amassed a collection of more than 10,000 anatomical specimens, all of which were initially housed at his Leicester Square residence. He has been called the "father of scientific surgery."

A little way down, the Moon Under Water pub stands on the site of:

3. **28 Leicester Square,** where John Singleton Copley, a leading portrait painter, lived with his family from 1776 to 1783. On December 5, 1782, while Copley was working on a portrait of Elkanah Watson, the two adjourned in order to hurry over to the House of Lords to hear George III announce the end of the American War of Independence. On their return, Watson said that Copley, "with a bold hand, a master's touch, and I believe an American heart," painted the stars and stripes on the flag flying from a ship in the background of the portrait. Watson later observed: "This, I imagine, was the first American flag hoisted in England."

   When you reach Hogarth Gate (where you entered the gardens), walk past the red phone box and proceed ahead into Leicester Place, which was laid out and constructed in the 1790s. Half a block ahead, on your right, is:

4. **Notre Dame de France,** 5 Leicester Place, a skylight-topped round church founded by a Marist priest in 1865. The facade features a statue of Mater Misericordia, while the carved pillars and reliefs portray eight scenes from the life of the Virgin Mary, all created by students from Paris's Ecole des Beaux-Arts. Inside, you'll find an unassuming altar made of Portland stone. The murals in the Blessed Sacrament Chapel, to your left, were painted in 1960 by Jean Cocteau; they depict the Annunciation, Mary at the foot of the cross, and the Assumption.

   Exit the church, continue to the end of Leicester Place, and turn right onto:

5. **Lisle Street,** one of half a dozen streets just north of Leicester Square that comprise London's Chinatown. A stroll here will reveal block after block of Chinese restaurants, grocers, and herbalists. Once concentrated in the Docklands area east of the city, London's Chinese community—then numbering some 2,000—began to migrate westward in the 1950s, seeking out new business opportunities. Chinese restaurants first opened in Soho after World War II to cater to British servicemen who had acquired a taste for Chinese food overseas. At the time, Soho was dominated by shabby brothels, seedy nightclubs, and run-down eating places. Because short-term

leases could be obtained for rather modest sums, Chinese entrepreneurs began renting properties in this area, and Chinatown was born. Today there are many good, inexpensive Chinese restaurants here, most specializing in traditional Cantonese cuisine.

Continue right along Lisle Street; at the corner of Newport Place is the:

6. **West Central,** 30 Lisle St. Formerly called the White Bear, this tavern hosted some of the earliest Rolling Stones rehearsals in 1962; their appearance was arranged by Brian Jones.

Turn left onto Newport Place, and then turn left again under the Chinatown arch onto Gerrard Street—the bustling, colorful center of London's Chinatown. A few doors down, on your left, is:

7. **Loon Fung Supermarket,** 42–44 Gerrard St., a large Chinese market selling exotic foods. Poet John Dryden (1631–1700) once lived unhappily with his wife in a house on this site. When Dryden's wife commented that she'd like to be a book so that the writer would pay more attention to her, Dryden replied, "Pray my dear . . . let it be an almanac, for then I shall change you every year." Reflecting further on his marriage, Dryden penned the following premature epitaph (she ended up outliving him):

> *Here lies my wife, so let her lie*
> *Now she's at rest and so am I.*

Continue to the end of Gerrard Street, passing the two carved stone **Chinese lions** on your left (a donation from the People's Republic of China in 1985). Just beyond, and also on the left, notice the two Chinese-style pagoda **telephone boxes.**

At the intersection with Wardour Street, turn right, cross Shaftesbury Avenue, and continue straight to the iron gates (on the right) that guard:

8. **St. Anne's Church Tower.** An entire church once stood here, built by Sir Christopher Wren in 1678, and dedicated to Queen Anne by her tutor, Henry Compton. The chapel was destroyed by World War II bombs, and all that

remains today is this peculiar beer-barrel–shaped church tower, designed by architect Samuel Pepys Cockerell.

Walk through the gates and stand by the tower. Above the large tombstone on the wall to your right is a tablet commemorating Theodore, king of Corsica, "who died in this parish December 11, 1756." Forced from his kingdom, Theodore sought asylum in London but was soon imprisoned here for debt. Writer Horace Walpole composed the following epitaph for the king:

> *The grave, great teacher to a level brings*
> *heroes and beggars, galley slaves and kings*
> *but Theodore this moral learn ere dead*
> *fate poured its lessons on his living head*
> *bestowed a Kingdom and denied him bread.*

Exit the churchyard through the gates you entered, turn right on Wardour Street, and turn right again onto:

9. **Old Compton Street,** Soho's main shopping thoroughfare. This street was named for Henry Compton, former Bishop of London. Today, Old Compton is very popular with London's gay community. Lining the street are numerous cafes where patrons can dine alfresco as Soho's colorful street life drifts by.

   Cross Old Compton Street, turn right, and then take the first left onto Dean Street. Keeping to the left side, continue to the corner of:

10. **Meard Street,** a short street that was a private project of carpenter John Meard—on the rowhouse wall, you can still see a plaque inscribed MEARDS STREET 1732.

    Continue a short distance down Dean Street until you arrive on the right at:

11. **Leoni's Quo Vadis,** 26–29 Dean St. (© **020/7437-9585**), a restaurant established by P. G. Leoni in 1926. Before it was a restaurant, this building was the home of Karl Marx. He and his family lived in two small upstairs rooms from 1851 to 1856, subsisting on a small weekly sum given to them by their friend Friedrich Engels. Marx claimed that he rarely went out "because my clothes are in pawn." Three of his young children died here.

Backtrack along Dean Street and take the first left onto Bateman Street. At the intersection with Frith Street, on the left, you'll find the:

Take a Break **Dog and Duck Public House,** 18 Bateman St, which has stood on this site since 1734; the pub's name recalls the rather cruel sport of duck hunting, which had been popular when the area was more rural. Today, this is the quintessential locals' pub in Soho. George Orwell chose to celebrate in this pub when the American Book-of-the-Month Club selected his *Animal Farm* as its book of the month.

Exit the pub right onto:

12. **Frith Street.** Initially named for its builder, Richard Frith, this commercial street was called Thrift Street for a time; around the turn of the century, its original name was restored.

Continue along Frith Street for a half block. On your left, you'll see the stage entrance of the Prince Edward Theatre. This building stands on the site of a former residence of Wolfgang Amadeus Mozart:

13. **Wolfgang Amadeus Mozart House,** 20 Frith St. Mozart (1756–91) was already a renowned prodigy (age 8) when his family came here to stay for 6 months. A local celebrity, Mozart attracted attention whenever he and his sister took walks around the neighborhood. The young composer gave a recital of his own works in his lodgings here, performing on a miniature violin that was specially made for him.

A little farther along, the attic of what is now Bar Italia was formerly:

14. **John Logie Baird's House,** 22 Frith St. Baird (1888–1946), a poverty-stricken inventor, was a sick man when he moved into the upper floors of this building in 1925. On October 2 of that year, he transmitted the first television picture—it was of his odd-job boy, William Taynton. In the spring of 1926, he invited members of the Royal Institute here to witness his new invention. He sold his system to the BBC, but unfortunately for him, it elected to use another system.

Retrace your steps along Frith Street for 1 block until, on the right, you arrive at:

15. **Hazlitt's Hotel,** 6 Frith St. This building dates from 1718 and is named for essayist William Hazlitt (1778–1830), a Renaissance man who began as a painter but turned to writing essays for popular critical magazines. Hazlitt died in this building with these words: "Well, I've had a happy life."

    Continue to the end of Frith Street. On your left, you'll pass the London headquarters of Twentieth Century Fox. Frith Street opens onto:

16. **Soho Square,** an attractive, quiet square that somehow seems out of place amid the theaters, clubs, and shops just a few steps away. Laid out during the reign of Charles II, the square became home to the Duke of Monmouth, the king's illegitimate son. Monmouth used "Soho" as his secret password at the Battle of Sedgemoor in 1685, where he met defeat in his attempt to oust Charles's successor, James II. Many of his co-conspirators were executed in what became known as the Bloody Assizes; the duke himself was tried and later beheaded at the Tower of London.

    The small black-and-white **wooden structure** at the center of the square is a tollhouse dating from the 1870s. Also in the square's gardens is a **statue of Charles II,** dating from 1681.

    Walking counterclockwise around the square, stop at the corner of Greek Street to see the:

17. **House of St. Barnabus,** 1 Greek St. (✆ **020/7437-1894**), believed to have been the inspiration for Dr. Manette's house in Charles Dickens's *A Tale of Two Cities.* The mid-18th-century house is noted for its extraordinarily detailed interior, complete with carved wood, rococo plasterwork, and a wrought-iron staircase. Now serving as a temporary shelter for homeless women, the house is open to the public on the first Monday of each month from 10am to 4pm. There is no need to book a tour; just turn up at the chapel door.

Continue to walk around the square counterclockwise. Once over Soho Street you'll come to:

18. **10 Soho Square,** a late-17th-century building that was once the home of Lady Mary Wortley Montague, a gifted intellectual and writer. She was a leader of society and fashion, and the friend (or enemy) of most of the literary figures of her time. Her contemporary, Horace Walpole, once described her as "old, foul, tawdry, painted, plastered. . . . She wears a foul mop that does not cover her greasy black locks that hang loose, never combed, never curled." Lady Mary might have married poet Alexander Pope, except that when he proposed, she laughed so long and loud that he immediately became one of her enemies.

The redbrick building next door is the:

19. **French Protestant Church,** erected in the 16th century "in grateful memory of H. M. King Edward VI who, by his charter of 1550, granted asylum to the Huguenots from France."

Continue on to:

20. **1 Soho Square,** home of MPL Industries, the former Beatle Sir Paul McCartney's London office.

Exit Soho Square by turning right onto Carlisle Street. Three hundred years ago, here stood the:

21. **Home of the Earl of Carlisle.** The Earl of Carlisle was friends with an eccentric inventor named Joseph Merlin, who, in the 1760s, was working on what became his most notable invention: roller skates. One evening, during an elegant ball, the unorthodox Merlin demonstrated his skates by rolling at high speed through the mansion's salon while playing the violin. Losing his balance, he crashed through an ornate—and very expensive—mirror, thus ending the demonstration and the ball.

Continue along Carlisle Street, turn left onto Dean Street, and then turn right onto the pedestrian St. Anne's Court. One block down on your right is:

22. **17 St. Anne's Court,** a gray building that once housed the studio where the Beatles recorded several tracks of *The White Album* and "Hey Jude." The studio's grand piano was auctioned in 1989 for £30,000.

From St. Anne's Court, bear left across Wardour Street (home of many of London's most important film companies) and walk straight onto Broadwick Street. Just ahead, at the corner of Poland Street, is the:

23. **Broadwick Street Pump,** a water pump that was identified by Dr. John Snow (1813–58) as the source of the 1854 Soho cholera epidemic. Snow, a noted anesthetist who had studied cholera during a previous epidemic, theorized that polluted drinking water caused the disease. He plotted on a map the addresses of more than 500 people who died in September 1854, and discovered that the Broad Street Public Water Pump (as it was then called) was at the geographic center of the epidemic. Snow's theory initially met with disbelief, but when the doctor had the handle of the pump removed, preventing it from being used, the outbreak soon ended.

    Continue past the row of elegant 18th-century houses and walk to the end of Broadwick Street to turn left onto:

24. **Carnaby Street,** London's "fashion" center in the 1960s. This pedestrian-only thoroughfare was laid out in the 1680s and named for Karnaby House, an apartment complex that housed a large number of Huguenot immigrants. The area slowly changed, and by the mid–19th century the street was home to tradespeople who owned neighborhood shops. In 1957, retailers John Stephens, John Vince, and Andreas Spyropoulus opened Carnaby Street's first boutique: a men's store that soon attracted other fashionable-clothing shops. In the 1960s, Carnaby Street became synonymous with "flower power." *Time* magazine focused international attention on the street, and the *Oxford English Dictionary* defined Carnaby Street as "fashionable clothing for young people."

    Today, the world of high fashion has moved elsewhere, but Carnaby Street still has a number of clothing shops that are worth looking at.

    At the end of Carnaby Street, turn left into Beak Street. A little way along, on the left, you'll come to:

25. **41 Beak St.,** home of Italian painter Antonio Canaletto (1697–1768) from 1749 to 1751. While living here, he advertised that he had a painting of his for sale, *A View of*

St. James's Park, that would "be shown to any gentleman that will be pleased to come to his house."

Cross Beak Street, go along Upper John Street, and turn right into:

26. **Golden Square.** In the middle of the square you'll find a **statue of George II** (1683–1760) by an unknown sculptor. There is an intriguing tale about how the statue came to the square: It was being auctioned when an old friend of the auctioneer walked in and nodded a greeting to him. The price of his unintentional purchase was so low as to be inconsequential, so the man accepted it and later presented it to Golden Square. Though few of the square's original buildings survive, if you proceed counterclockwise, **nos. 23 and 24** (home to the Portuguese Embassy from 1724–47) give an impression of what the square would have looked like in the 18th century.

Once past these buildings, continue into Lower James Street, pausing to look at the modern redbrick building on the square's south side. This building stands on the site of:

27. **14 Golden Square,** where Thomas Jefferson leased rooms on March 11, 1786. John Adams had urged Jefferson to come to London from Paris. The two statesmen hoped to take advantage of the presence of the ambassador of Tripolitania in London in order to resolve the issue of American ships being seized by Barbary Coast pirates. After a month of attending to diplomatic and social functions, Jefferson left for home with some relief. As he said to a friend: "This nation hates us, their ministers hate us, and their king more than any other man."

A little way down Lower John Street, notice the narrow building that's second along on the left:

28. **4 Lower John St.** This building, which was erected around 1685, was designed to have just one room on each floor.

Turn left into Brewer Street and take the third left into Great Pultney Street. A little way down, on the left, pause outside the former home of:

29. **John William Polidori,** 38 Great Pultney St. Having received his medical degree from Edinburgh University in

1815, Polidori (1795–1821) was hired in March 1816 as the personal physician to Lord Byron when the poet left England for exile in Europe. The young doctor idolized Byron and hoped that Byron would help him begin his own literary career. But when Polidori showed his writing to Byron, the poet mocked it and told him he would never make it as a writer. In the summer of 1816, during their stay at Lake Geneva, Byron conceived the idea of a ghost-story competition (a challenge that gave birth to Mary Shelley's *Frankenstein*). Polidori wrote two stories, one of which, *The Vampyre*, is now acknowledged as one of the most influential pieces of Gothic literature. Polidori's prose presented the vampire as a seductive, mobile, noble, and erotic creature, recognizably human, with pale skin and cold eyes. More than half a century later, Polidori's story would inspire Bram Stoker to write *Dracula*.

After Byron dismissed him, Polidori returned to England to find that the *New Monthly Magazine* had published *The Vampyre* and attributed it to Lord Byron. He wrote to the editor asking that the error of authorship be corrected, only to find himself branded a plagiarist. The charge all but destroyed his literary reputation and, in 1821, he finally gave up writing and enrolled as a law student. On August 24 of that year, in his house here in Great Pultney Street, he took his own life by drinking prussic acid.

Backtrack to Brewer Street and turn left. From this point, the street epitomizes the essence of Soho, lined as it is with an incredible variety of shops, from peep shows and hostess bars to traditional village shops.

Somewhat farther along Brewer Street you'll arrive on the left at:

Take a Break   **Randall and Aubin,** 16 Brewer St. This lively and noisy eatery, specializing in seafood, occupies premises that have changed little since opening as a delicatessen in 1911.

Continue walking along Brewer Street; take the first right turn into Rupert Street, and proceed to Shaftesbury Avenue. Turn right and continue ahead to Piccadilly Circus Underground Station.

Chelsea

Start: Sloane Square Underground Station.

Finish: Sloane Square Underground Station.

Time: 2½ hours.

Best Times: Monday to Saturday from 10am to noon and from 2 to 4pm. Also, Sunday from 2 to 4pm, when the interiors on the tour are open. Saturday on King's Road is particularly lively.

Worst Times: At night and on Sunday morning (when most shops on King's Road are closed).

Chelsea today is an incredibly expensive residential area, but that wasn't always the case. Stretching along the Thames, south of Hyde Park and Kensington, Chelsea gained fame in the 19th century as London's Bohemia, a place full of writers, artists, musicians, and thinkers. This beautiful "town within a city" was home to Thomas Carlyle, George Eliot, J. M. W. Turner, John Singer Sargent, Oscar Wilde, Henry James—the list of famous former residents seems endless.

In the 20th century Chelsea was discovered by a new group of Londoners—its location and beauty have turned it into a favorite stomping ground of the monied classes. This tour will take you through one of the world's most beguiling urban neighborhoods.

• • • • • • • • • • • • • • • • •

Exit Sloane Square Underground Station, turn right, and walk a few steps to the:

1. **Royal Court Theatre,** Sloane Square (© **020/7565-5000**). Opened in 1888, the Royal Court quickly gained a top reputation by staging George Bernard Shaw's plays, many of which were rehearsed and performed here under his personal direction. After serving as a cinema in the 1930s and suffering bomb damage during World War II, the theater was rebuilt and became home to the English Stage Company—one of the city's most innovative theatrical groups. With the premiere of John Osborne's *Look Back in Anger* in 1956, the Royal Court became the place where many important and innovative playwrights made their debuts. The theater is known for consistently high-quality productions.

Buy a ticket for the evening's performance, and then retrace your steps past Sloane Square Station. Continue straight ahead to:

2. **Sloane Gardens,** named for Sir Hans Sloane (1660–1753), who served as president of the Royal Society for 14 years. Sloane, who lived nearby, gained fame for his collection of more than 800 plant and animal specimens, which he kept in his home. Upon his death, he bequeathed 50,000 books and thousands of manuscripts to the British Museum—a windfall for its emerging collection.

The magnificent redbrick houses lining both sides of Sloane Gardens were built by developer/parliamentarian William Willett, who, incidentally, was the chief campaigner for the establishment of summer time (daylight savings time) in 1889.

Located just after the bend in the street is:

3. **49 Sloane Gardens,** the former home of novelist/dramatist Egerton Castle (1858–1926), who lived here during the last years of his life.

Chelsea

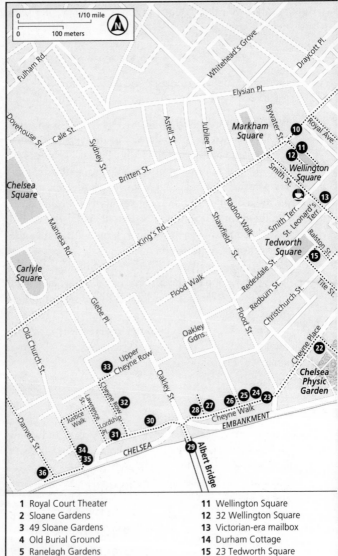

1 Royal Court Theater
2 Sloane Gardens
3 49 Sloane Gardens
4 Old Burial Ground
5 Ranelagh Gardens
6 Chelsea Royal Hospital
7 Duke of York's Headquarters
8 Royal Avenue
9 18 St. Leonard's Terrace
10 King's Road

11 Wellington Square
12 32 Wellington Square
13 Victorian-era mailbox
14 Durham Cottage
15 23 Tedworth Square
16 34 Tite St.
17 31 Tite St.
18 33 Tite St.
19 Whitehouse
20 Paradise Walk

21 Clover Mews
22 Chelsea Physic Garden
23 Cheyne Walk
24 2 Cheyne Walk
25 4 Cheyne Walk
26 6 Cheyne Walk
27 16 Cheyne Walk
28 Cheyne Mews
29 Albert Bridge
30 48 Cheyne Walk

31 Carlyle Mansions
32 24 Cheyne Row
33 22 Upper Cheyne Row
34 Chelsea Old Church
35 Statue of Sir Thomas More
36 Crosby Hall

At the end of Sloane Gardens, turn left onto the busier Lower Sloane Street. Continue 2 blocks, past the upscale shops, down to the traffic lights, and go right into Royal Hospital Road, where immediately on the left is the:

4. **Old Burial Ground,** the cemetery of the adjacent Chelsea Royal Hospital (see stop 6). Alas, the cemetery isn't open to the public, but you can see almost everything through the surrounding iron railings. Though there are not many tombstones, the cemetery is believed to be the final resting place of more than 10,000 former soldiers. A soldier, Simon Box, was the first to be buried here, in 1692. Two of the more unusual stones are those of Robert Cumming and Joshua Cueman, which claim that at their deaths—in the 18th century—the men were aged 116 and 123, respectively. William Hiseland's 1732 headstone says that he was in the army for 80 years and "when a hundred years old he took unto him a wife." (It would appear that the Chelsea Royal Hospital was extremely successful in preserving the lives of its occupants.) Two women are interred here, Christian David and Hanah Bell; both followed their lovers into battle in the Crimean War, disguised as male soldiers. Their secrets weren't discovered until they were wounded in action.

For lack of additional burial space, the Old Burial Ground had to close in 1854.

Continue along Royal Hospital Road with the cemetery to your left. After about 91m (300 ft.), turn left and pass through the gates. Walk through Garden Gate and enter, on your left, the:

5. **Ranelagh Gardens,** one of 18th-century London's favorite outdoor areas. From 1742 to 1805, Ranelagh was the site of the Great Rotunda, an amusement park and meeting place for the upper classes. Eighteenth-century politician and man of letters Horace Walpole wrote, "Every night constantly I go to Ranelagh . . . my Lord Chesterfield is so fond of it that he says he has ordered all his letters to be directed thither." Gently sloping toward the Thames, the wooded and flowered greens of Ranelagh are some of the prettiest in London and a pleasure to stroll. Today the Royal Hospital, which looms over the

gardens, is the only remaining building in this park. The gates you entered are this park's only entrance; they close daily from 1 to 2pm.

Leave the gardens and turn right. Retrace your steps through Garden Gate, turn left into the driveway, and walk straight through the wooden doors into the central court of the:

6. **Chelsea Royal Hospital.** Designed by Sir Christopher Wren (architect of St. Paul's Cathedral), the hospital was founded in 1682 by Charles II for men "broken by war and old age." Inspired by the Hôtel des Invalides in Paris, the Chelsea Royal Hospital still serves as a home for elderly, unmarried war veterans with no other sources of income. Today there are about 420 "Chelsea pensioners," male veterans over the age of 65 who receive food, shelter, and clothing, plus a small weekly allowance, which they happily supplement by showing visitors around the buildings. You can easily identify the pensioners by the scarlet or blue uniforms and tricornered hats that they wear on special occasions.

Walk past the **statue of Charles II** and enter the hospital through the main door, under the clock. On your right is the **chapel,** featuring a relatively bright interior that's typical of Wren churches. On your left is the **Great Hall,** an awe-inspiring, wood-paneled dining room that would probably transform even the most mundane meal into an exquisite banquet. The painting on the left wall is of Charles II on horseback.

The Chelsea Royal Hospital is open to the public Monday to Saturday from 10am to noon and 2 to 4pm and Sunday from 2 to 4pm.

Return to Royal Hospital Road, cross the pedestrian walkway, and continue straight ahead on Franklin's Row. With the private cricket grounds and tennis courts on your left, walk 1 block to the:

7. **Duke of York's Headquarters,** the large compound on your right, surrounded by an iron railing. Now used as a barracks for the Territorial Army—England's National Guard—the complex was built in 1801 as a school for war-orphaned children. The duke for whom this property

was named was the second son of George III and the head of the English army. The Duke of York earned a reputation as a military reformer because he tried to stop the widespread buying and selling of army commissions. The number of officers who were unfit for their positions had grown so large that the duke finally asked for the resignations of all colonels under age 20 and all captains under age 12. Ironically, it was later discovered that the duke's mistress was one of the people who were selling commissions, and he was forced to resign in disgrace. The Duke of York's Headquarters isn't open to the public.

Turn left onto St. Leonard's Terrace and walk 1 block to arrive at:

8. **Royal Avenue,** a romantically quiet and picturesque street lined with tall brick homes from the early 19th century. The street was laid out in 1682 by Sir Christopher Wren; he intended it to be part of a direct route from the Chelsea Royal Hospital to Kensington Palace. However, this short block was the only part of the project that had been completed by 1685, when Charles II, the plan's sponsor, died. The rest of the route was never finished.

Continue along St. Leonard's Terrace to the row of houses on the right, where a blue plaque at:

9. **18 St. Leonard's Terrace** commemorates the former home of Bram Stoker (1847–1912). A prolific author, Stoker moved here in 1896, the year before his most famous book, *Dracula,* was published.

Retrace your footsteps to turn left into Royal Avenue. Continue to its end and turn left onto:

10. **King's Road,** Chelsea's primary commercial thoroughfare. Laid out in the 17th century, this was originally the king's road—a private street built exclusively for Charles II, enabling him to travel from his London home to Hampton Court Palace. The only people allowed to use this road were the king and holders of a special copper pass with a crown on one side and the words "The King's Private Road" on the other. King's Road remained private until the 1830s. Now celebrated for its shops and boutiques, this is one of London's best shopping streets. It's

especially crowded on Saturdays, when the city's trendiest young people transform it into an informal fashion show.

Walk 1 block and turn left into:

11. **Wellington Square,** a delightfully picturesque horse-shoe named for the Duke of Wellington. Built around 1830, the square has been home to several famous residents, including A. A. Milne (1882–1956), creator of Winnie-the-Pooh, who lived at no. 8 from 1904 to 1906, in what he later described as "two cheap and dirty rooms" at the top of the house. (Milne also lived nearby, on Mallord Street, for almost 30 years.) While living on Wellington Square, Milne wrote his first book, *Lovers in London.*

Walk around the square to no. 30. This was the presumed home of fictional hero James Bond, though not specifically pinpointed by his creator, Ian Fleming. Close by you'll see:

12. **32 Wellington Square,** where American novelist Thomas Wolfe (1900–38) lived for a year, during which he wrote *Look Homeward, Angel,* one of his best-known works.

Back on King's Road, turn left, walk 1 block, and turn left onto Smith Street. On the next corner:

☕ **Take a Break** **The Resident,** 23 Smith St., is a good place to take a tipple with the locals. There are always special rotating guest beers, as well as the popular brands. Food choices include sausages, sandwiches, pasta, vegetarian dishes, and hot meat pies.

Continue 1 block down Smith Street where, at the corner of St. Leonard's Terrace, you'll see a:

13. **Victorian-era mailbox.** Shaped like a pillar, the thickly painted red box incorporates the Royal Badge (a lion and a unicorn) and the initials VR (for Victoria Regina) above an extremely narrow mail slot.

Cross over St. Leonard's Terrace and go straight into Durham Place. Take the first right into Christchurch Street where, set back from the road on the right, you'll find:

14. **Durham Cottage,** 4 Christchurch St., the former home of Sir Laurence Olivier and Vivien Leigh, who scandalized polite society by becoming involved while they were both still married to others. They moved here in May 1937, and Vivien set about decorating and furnishing the house in Regency style, complete with antiques and artworks. One observer thought that the house possessed an "almost claustrophobic prettiness," with Olivier relegated to the role of "an unfortunate bull in a china shop."

    On November 5, 1938, the couple invited Ralph Richardson and his wife here to celebrate Vivien's birthday. Since it was also Guy Fawkes night, Richardson arrived with a box of fireworks and went into the garden to set off a rocket. Alas, a firecracker flew straight back into the dining room, burning new curtains (of which Vivien was extremely proud) and destroying antique crockery. Vivien was furious; Richardson summoned his wife and attempted to leave, but as he reached the door, the handle came off in his hand.

    Continue along Christchurch Street and take the next right into Ralston Street. Take the first left into Tedworth Square, and on the next corner you will find:

15. **23 Tedworth Square,** the former home of Mark Twain (Samuel Langhorne Clemens, 1835–1910). Twain gained fame and fortune writing such American classics as *The Adventures of Tom Sawyer* (1873) and *The Adventures of Huckleberry Finn* (1885). However, he lived extravagantly and invested poorly; thus, in 1891, the bankrupt Twain fled to Europe to escape his creditors. After his daughter, Susy, died in August 1896, Twain secluded himself in this house. The following year, the *New York Herald* newspaper set up a fund to collect money to repay Twain's debts, enabling his return to America.

    Turn left into Tite Street and, keeping to the right side, walk to the pedestrian crossing, go over Royal Hospital Road, and continue ahead. A little way along on the right is:

16. **34 Tite St.,** the former home of Oscar Wilde (1854–1900). When the controversial Irish wit and dramatist moved here in 1885, he was already a celebrity,

the author of such works as *The Importance of Being Earnest* and *The Picture of Dorian Gray*. Wilde lived here for 10 years. It was here, in 1891, that Wilde was introduced to his lover, Lord Alfred Douglas (known as Bosie), son of the Marquess of Queensberry. Douglas's father disapproved of their relationship, even going so far as to once turn up here carrying a horsewhip, intent on thrashing Wilde.

Wilde was later prosecuted as a homosexual, then a criminal offense. The authorities gave him time to leave the country, but the defiant Wilde chose instead to sip champagne at the nearby Cadogan Hotel, where he was arrested. Upon conviction, Wilde was sentenced to 2 years of hard labor. After being released, he went into exile in Paris, where he died in poverty in 1900.

Continue half a block farther down Tite Street where, on the left side, you will find:

17. **31 Tite St.,** the former home of John Singer Sargent (1856–1925). The American artist lived and worked in this house until his death on April 15, 1925.

    Next door is:

18. **33 Tite St.,** the former studio of Augustus John (1879–1961). One of the best-loved Welsh portraitists, John was a founding member of the De Stijl movement, which emphasized pure abstraction and simplicity. The bearded, charismatic painter epitomized the English bohemian of the 1950s, defying social convention in his dress, behavior, and way of life. An infamous womanizer, John attracted and mistreated numerous women.

    Continue to the light-brown brick building (with the lantern over the black door) next door. This was once the site of the:

19. **Whitehouse,** a grand home built in the 1870s for American painter James Abbott McNeill Whistler (1834–1903). While the house was still under construction, Whistler brought a slander suit against art critic John Ruskin because of his review of Whistler's painting *Nocturne in Black and Gold: The Falling Rocket*. Ruskin wrote: "I never expected to hear a coxcomb ask 200

guineas for flinging a pot of paint in the public's face." Though Whistler won the case, he was awarded only one farthing (a quarter-cent) in damages and was ordered to pay his own enormous legal costs. Temporarily bankrupt, the painter was forced to sell his beloved Whitehouse.

Turn right onto Dilke Street and right again onto:

20. **Paradise Walk,** a tranquil block lined with a pretty row of cottages trimmed with shuttered windows. The street wasn't always this bucolic, however; in the late 19th century, it was such a slum that Oscar Wilde erected a screen in his backyard so that he wouldn't have to look at it.

Return to Dilke Street and take the next right onto:

21. **Clover Mews,** another pretty street that helps make Chelsea one of London's most desirable neighborhoods. The word *mews* comes from the French word *muer* ("to molt"). Originally a place where hawks were kept while molting, mews evolved to become buildings with stables on the ground floor and living quarters upstairs. Eventually, mews referred to the small streets where such buildings were located.

Return to Dilke Street and take the next right onto Swan Walk. Look through the iron gate on your left at the:

22. **Chelsea Physic Garden** (✆ 020/7352-5646), the second-oldest physic garden in England (the one in Oxford is older). Originally established by the Apothecaries' Company in 1673 as a place to cultivate medicinal plants, the garden has since expanded to include species from the New World. Behind its high walls resides a rare collection of exotic plants, shrubs, and trees—many of them more than 100 years old. An unusual rock garden features stone from the Tower of London and basaltic lava from Iceland. In 1732, cottonseeds were sent from this garden to American colonist James Oglethorpe, who planted some of the first cotton crops in his Georgia colony; these succeeded so well that cotton plantations—and the slavery economy employed to operate them—would soon dominate much of the rural American South.

The garden is open April to October only, Wednesday from 2 to 5pm, and Sunday from 2 to 6pm. The resident

English Gardening School holds lectures throughout the summer. Call for details.

Turn left around the gardens to Cheyne Place; after 2 blocks, bear right (across Flood St.) onto:

23. **Cheyne Walk,** one of the most celebrated streets in Chelsea. The houses on Cheyne (rhymes with rainy) were built in 1720 and have been owned by famous people in the arts and entertainment field for more than a century.

    A few steps ahead is:

24. **2 Cheyne Walk,** a house that John Barrymore leased in November 1924. Barrymore had just finished performing *Hamlet* in New York, and decided to try the role before London audiences. He couldn't find an English producer willing to take a chance on an American actor in this role, so Barrymore financed the production himself. He leased the Haymarket Theatre, and the play opened on February 19, 1925. In the audience on opening night were such luminaries as John Masefield, Somerset Maugham, Arnold Bennett, and George Bernard Shaw. The drama critic of the *Sunday Times* praised Barrymore's performance thus: "We know ourselves to be in the presence of a fine and powerful mind."

    Just beyond, you'll come to:

25. **4 Cheyne Walk,** the former home of novelist George Eliot (Mary Ann Evans, 1819–80). Throughout much of her life, Eliot was enveloped in scandal for living with a married man, literary critic George Henry Lewes. Often treated as a social pariah, Eliot found it extremely uncomfortable to appear in public with her lover. After Lewes died in 1878, Eliot became involved with John Cross, whom she later married. The couple moved to this house in 1880, but their time together was short because Eliot died just a few months later, in December 1880. On his wife's death, Cross wrote in his diary, " . . . and I am left alone in this new house we were meant to be so happy in."

    Two doors down, at:

26. **6 Cheyne Walk,** you can see an excellent, well-preserved example of the block's original 1720s architecture.

One block ahead is:

27. **16 Cheyne Walk,** the former home of Dante Gabriel Rossetti (1828–82). The 19th-century pre-Raphaelite painter/poet lived and worked in this handsome Tudor house from 1862 until his death. He moved here soon after the death of his wife, Elizabeth Siddal. As she was buried, the distraught Rossetti had a volume of his love poetry wrapped in her long hair and entombed with her. Seven years later, however, he had second thoughts about his romantic gesture, exhumed the manuscript, and published the poems.

    Quite the eccentric, Rossetti turned his home into a sort of menagerie, filling it with a collection of exotic animals. In addition to a kangaroo and a raccoon, the artist kept a white bull whose antics turned the garden into a wasteland. He also kept a wombat that was much admired by his friend Lewis Carroll (Charles Dodgson); in fact, it inspired Carroll to create the dormouse for *Alice in Wonderland*.

    Continue ahead and turn right into:

28. **Cheyne Mews,** where a tunnel runs between nos. 23 and 24 Cheyne Walk. Henry VIII's country house stood here until 1753, when it was demolished following the death of its last occupant, Sir Hans Sloane (see stop 2). The cautionary sign at the entrance to the tunnel on your left reads: ALL DRIVERS OF VEHICLES ARE DIRECTED TO *walk* THEIR HORSES WHILE PASSING UNDER THIS ARCHWAY.

    Return to Cheyne Walk and continue to the corner of Oakley Street. On your left you'll see:

29. **Albert Bridge,** one of the most picturesque spans in the world. Constructed at the height of the Victorian fascination with cast iron, it was designed in 1873 by R. M. Ordish.

    Cross Oakley Street and continue along Cheyne Walk, pausing to admire one of London's most graceful statues, David Wynne's *Boy with a Dolphin*. One block ahead on your right is:

30. **48 Cheyne Walk,** the former home of Rolling Stones lead singer Mick Jagger, who lived here in the early 1970s. Band member Charlie Watts still lives nearby.

Continue along Cheyne Row, where a little way along on the right you will find:

31. **Carlyle Mansions,** where the newly married Ian Fleming leased a third-floor river-view apartment in 1952. Fleming jested that he'd started writing novels in order to overcome the shock of getting married at the age of 44. Although he began work on *Casino Royale* while on the island of Jamaica, he revised it in his apartment here. He derived his hero's name, James Bond, from the name of an ornithologist whose volume on birds sat on his breakfast table.

Backtrack along Cheyne Walk and turn left into Cheyne Row; walk half a block to:

32. **24 Cheyne Row** (© 020/7352-7087), the beautifully preserved former residence of Thomas Carlyle (1795–1881), one of Britain's most important essayists and historians. Carlyle lived here a long time—from 1834 until his death. The house, dating from 1702, is now a museum administered by the National Trust. It's maintained much as it was in Carlyle's day, when the address was 5 Cheyne Row (notice that the 5 has been crossed out). There are still no electric lights on the upper floors.

While living here, Carlyle completed his epic *History of the French Revolution.* He lent the only manuscript of the first volume to John Stuart Mill, who shortly thereafter hurried to Carlyle's door to confess that his maid had "taken it for waste paper" and burned it. Carlyle was forced to rewrite the entire volume from memory, confessing at the end that he felt like a man who had "nearly killed himself accomplishing zero." A visit to this house is a must—it is so little changed, and makes a remarkable contrast with the busy Embankment neighborhood. It's open April to the end of October from Wednesday to Sunday and bank holiday Mondays from 2pm to 5pm. There's an admission charge.

Walk half a block to the end of Cheyne Row and turn right onto Upper Cheyne Row; a few yards down on your left is:

33. **22 Upper Cheyne Row,** the former home of Leigh Hunt (1784–1859), an essayist/poet who lived here from

1833 to 1840. A contemporary and friend of poets Byron, Keats, and Shelley, Hunt loved Chelsea and once wrote about this neighborhood:

"The end of the world. The air of the neighboring river so refreshing and the quiet of the 'no thoroughfare' so full of repose that although our fortunes were at their worst, and my health almost of a piece with them, I felt for some weeks as if I could sit still for ever, embalmed in silence."

Retrace your steps to the corner of Cheyne Row and continue straight ahead, where the road curves left into Lawrence Street. Walk 1 block down Lawrence Street, turn right onto the narrow Justice Walk, and then turn left onto Old Church Street to the tall brick:

34. **Chelsea Old Church,** the parish church of Sir Thomas More (1478–1535). The building's beauty is diminished only by the heavy traffic outside and the fact that it and the surrounding area were heavily damaged by bombs during World War II. Gracefully repaired, the church features a chapel designed in part by Hans Holbein; an urn that contains the remains of Sir Hans Sloane (see stop 2), the man who owned most of Chelsea during the 1700s; and a plaque commemorating the life of American novelist Henry James, a longtime Chelsea resident who died nearby in 1916. The Lawrence Chapel is supposed to have been the scene of Henry VIII's secret marriage to Jane Seymour several days before their official marriage in 1536.

Outside the church, on the corner, is a:

35. **Statue of Sir Thomas More,** good friend and chancellor of Henry VIII. When Henry broke with the Roman Catholic church, More refused to accept the king as head of the Church of England—a stance for which he was subsequently beheaded on Tower Hill. More's story is depicted in the play and film *A Man for All Seasons.*

Cross Old Church Street. Keeping the Thames to your left, walk down the steps and through the sunken garden. Climb the steps at the other side of the garden, and cross Danvers Street. The white-stone churchlike building to the right is:

36. **Crosby Hall,** an ornate reception hall that was once part of the home of Sir John Crosby, a wealthy wool merchant, and was owned successively by Richard III and then Sir Thomas More. The hall was built in the early 1400s in Bishopsgate, within the City of London, and was transported here stone by stone in the early 1900s under the partial sponsorship of American-born Lady Nancy Astor. Today the hall is private property, and is not open to the public.

With your back to the river, walk up Danvers Street and turn right onto King's Road. From here you can take a leisurely .6km (1-mile) stroll back to Sloane Square Underground Station, pausing to quench your thirst at any of the numerous cafes and pubs along the King's Road, and stopping to admire the boutiques and shops. Or, you can catch bus no. 11 or 22 for the return trip to Sloane Square.

Hampstead

Start: Hampstead Underground Station.

Finish: Hampstead Underground Station.

Time: 3 hours at a leisurely pace (not including visit to building interiors).

Best Times: Tuesday to Sunday between noon and 5pm, when many of the interiors are likely to be open.

Worst Times: Monday and winter evenings.

London's most famous suburb, Hampstead gained fame as a 17th- and 18th-century spa resort. Situated on a ridge overlooking the City of London and the Thames, Hampstead is centered on a heath (318 hectares/ 785 acres of wild royal parkland) about 6.4km (4 miles) north of the center of London. Hampstead's spas had fallen into disrepair by the mid–18th century, but the heath, which was dedicated "to the use of the public forever" by a special act of Parliament in 1872, remained the traditional playground of the Londoner—the "'Appy 'Ampstead" of cockney legend. In addition to high-rent homes, a bright shopping street, and the heath, Hampstead's varied landscape includes formal park lands, woods, and ponds.

Hampstead

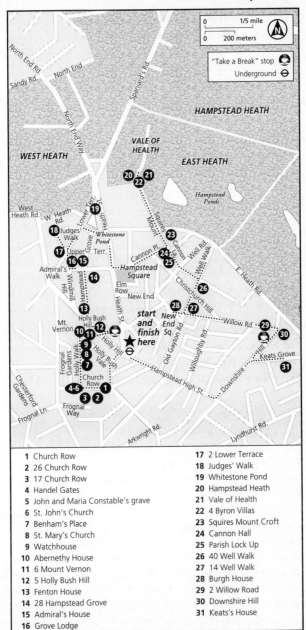

1 Church Row	**17** 2 Lower Terrace
2 26 Church Row	**18** Judges' Walk
3 17 Church Row	**19** Whitestone Pond
4 Handel Gates	**20** Hampstead Heath
5 John and Maria Constable's grave	**21** Vale of Health
6 St. John's Church	**22** 4 Byron Villas
7 Benham's Place	**23** Squires Mount Croft
8 St. Mary's Church	**24** Cannon Hall
9 Watchhouse	**25** Parish Lock Up
10 Abernethy House	**26** 40 Well Walk
11 6 Mount Vernon	**27** 14 Well Walk
12 5 Holly Bush Hill	**28** Burgh House
13 Fenton House	**29** 2 Willow Road
14 28 Hampstead Grove	**30** Downshire Hill
15 Admiral's House	**31** Keats's House
16 Grove Lodge	

"Leafy Hampstead," as it became known, has always attracted city dwellers eager to escape the grime and squalor of urban life, including such luminaries as landscape painter John Constable and poet John Keats. You are sure to enjoy strolling around one of England's loveliest pastures.

• • • • • • • • • • • • • • • • •

Exit Hampstead Underground Station and go straight ahead onto Heath Street. Continue until you reach a pedestrian crossing. Cross the road and you'll be at:

1. **Church Row,** often praised as one of the most attractive streets in Hampstead. Most of the carefully preserved houses on this block date from the 18th century and seem to be unspoiled by time. Walk down the left side of Church Row, noticing that an old lamp bracket remains on the corner, guarding the memory of its bygone gas lamp.

   A few doors down on your left is:

2. **26 Church Row,** the former home of Lord Alfred Douglas. Douglas (nicknamed Bosie) was the son of the Marquess of Queensberry, but was better known as Oscar Wilde's lover (for more information on Wilde, see stop 16 in Walking Tour 10).

   Farther along, on the same side, is:

3. **17 Church Row,** formerly the home of H. G. Wells (1866–1946), author of such farsighted, almost prophetic works as *The Time Machine, The Invisible Man, The War of the Worlds, The First Men in the Moon,* and *The War in the Air.*

   Continue straight ahead, toward St. John's Church, and enter through the wrought-iron church gates known as the:

4. **Handel Gates.** These gates came from Canon Park, Edgware, in 1747. It was there that George Frideric Handel served as composer for the Duke of Chandos.

   Enter through the left gate, turn immediately left, and follow the rough, unpaved path that runs past the aged gravestones. Walk all the way to the bottom and turn right onto the paved path. Behind an iron fence to your left is:

5. **John and Maria Constable's grave.** John Constable (1776–1837), one of England's greatest landscape painters, moved to Hampstead in 1819 so that his family "might enjoy fresher air than London could provide." Indeed, Hampstead provided Constable with much more than fresh air; it inspired him to create some of his best works. Over the next 15 years, he painted Hampstead's heath, houses, trees, and clouds. By his own admission, Constable's happiest years were spent in Hampstead, of which he said, "Here, let me take my everlasting rest."

   With your back to the gravestone, walk on the path through the bushes to:

6. **St. John's Church.** The present building, from 1745, rests on medieval foundations. When the structure was enlarged in the 19th century, the entire church was reoriented, making it one of the few churches in the city with an altar that faces west rather than east (the direction of Jerusalem).

   One hundred years ago, when the church's tower was facing possible demolition, it was saved only through the efforts of such locals as writer Anthony Trollope and artists William Morris and Holman Hunt.

   Enter the church's porch, which used to be the vestry. To your right are **tablets** listing the church's vicars, past and present. Directly ahead, on your left, is a bronze **bas-relief of Henry Cort.** According to Charles H. Morgan, the eminent American engineer who commissioned it, the bronze work honors the man "to whom the world is indebted for the arts of refining iron by paddling with mineral coal and of rolling metals in grooved rolls." Upon entering through the church's inner doors, you'll see a charming gray-wood interior. Before you go down the central aisle, look to the left at the proud old **font** with the carved figure of John the Baptist on top. Face the altar and look left to see the church's old **pulpit** on your left. Above the radiator, to the right of the altar, is a **bust of poet John Keats,** presented "to the English Nation" in 1894 by a group of his American admirers. Because Keats spent much of his life in Hampstead and wrote some of his finest works here, it was decided to place the statue in this church rather than in Westminster Abbey.

Climb the stairs to the right of Keats's bust. The small **cupboard** on your right was built to hold the loaves of bread that used to be given to the parish's poor. Turning left onto the balcony, you can stand in front of the church's **High Altar.**

Exit St. John's and walk down the pathway to your left. Go through the gates, cautiously cross the busy road, and walk straight ahead into Holly Walk. At the end of the graveyard, look to your right at:

7. **Benham's Place,** a quaint street lined with nine pretty cottages dating from 1813. These homes were built as part of a development undertaken by William Benham, a grocer and cheese seller on Hampstead High Street.

A few yards down Holly Walk, on your right, is:

8. **St. Mary's Church,** a 1796 chapel built by and for refugees who fled their homeland during the French Revolution. St. Mary's was one of the first Roman Catholic churches to open in London after the Reformation. Gen. Charles de Gaulle worshipped here during World War II.

Farther ahead on your right is the:

9. **Watchhouse,** 9 Holly Place, the 1830s headquarters of Hampstead's first police force. Not everyone was pleased with the new constabulary; many residents, including members of the local council, protested that police protection would place an undue burden on local taxpayers.

Step into Holly Berry Lane to savor its charm. Return to Holly Walk and turn right, then go right onto Mount Vernon to stop outside the first house on your right. This is:

10. **Abernethy House,** a former girls' school that became a lodging house in the late 19th century. Robert Louis Stevenson (1850–94), who wrote *Treasure Island, Kidnapped!,* and *Dr. Jekyll and Mr. Hyde,* stayed here several times. A booster of this charming suburb, Stevenson once remarked to a Scottish friend, "Hampstead is the most delightful place for air and scenery in London. I cannot understand how the air is so good, it does not explain itself to me."

Next door, at:

11. **6 Mount Vernon,** you can see a metal plaque above the front door. This is an insurance marker—proof that the house is covered by a fire company. Unlike modern insurance, late-18th-century policies didn't promise to repay any damage; instead, having insurance meant that if your house caught fire, the company you paid would come put it out!

At the end of Mount Vernon on the left is a **blue plaque** marking the home of physiologist Sir Henry Dale. Walk along the pathway across from Dale's house, keeping left around the bend. Cross Holly Hill onto Holly Mount. A short way down on the left side is the:

☕ **Take a Break** **Holly Bush Pub,** 22 Holly Mount, Heath Street. This tavern is closely associated with 18th-century painter George Romney (see below), who purchased several properties nearby in 1796. When his health failed a few years later, Romney returned to his estranged wife in the Lake District. His stables were leased out and converted into this delightful tavern, which offers good food served in several charming gas lamp–lit rooms. Burton and Tetley bitters are always on tap.

Leave the pub, turn left, and walk to the end of Holly Mount, where you'll be rewarded with a spectacular, though obstructed, view over London.

Backtrack down Holly Mount. Turn right onto Holly Bush Hill and walk five doors up to:

12. **5 Holly Bush Hill,** the former home of George Romney (1734–1802). A relatively well-to-do artist who moved here in 1796, Romney had deserted his wife several years earlier, proclaiming that "art and marriage do not mix." The artist's success as a portrait painter ended in 1797 (only a year after he had built this studio), owing to physical and mental illness. According to Romney's biographer, a friend noted in 1799 that his "increasing weakness of body and mind afforded only a gloomy prospect for the remainder of his life." Romney left Hampstead that year and returned to his wife in the Lake District, where he died a few years later.

The magnificent wrought-iron and gold-leaf gates across the street are the entrance to:

13. **Fenton House,** Windmill Hill ((© **020/7435-3471**), the oldest mansion in Hampstead, dating from 1693. Originally known as Ostend House, it was owned by silk merchant Joshua Gee (1667–1730), a man who had close American connections and who is known to have traded with George Washington's father. Gee imported pig iron from Maryland and became a landholder in Pennsylvania.

   Bequeathed to the National Trust in 1952, Fenton House now houses the Binning collection of furniture and porcelain (most of it dating from the 18th century), as well as the Benton Fletcher collection of early keyboard instruments (some of which you can still play).

   The house is open in March on Saturday and Sunday from 2 to 6pm, and from April to October Saturday to Wednesday from 11am to 6pm. There's an admission charge.

   The entrance to the house is located on Hampstead Grove, which begins to the right of the gates. From the entrance, continue a little way and, on the right, pause outside:

14. **28 Hampstead Grove,** formerly the home of George du Maurier (1834–96), grandfather of Daphne du Maurier. George du Maurier created the infamous character Svengali for his novel *Trilby.* His other works include *Peter Ibbetson* and *The Martian.* He was also a prolific artist (despite being almost blind in his left eye) and regularly contributed cartoons to the satirical magazine *Punch.*

   Continue uphill to turn left onto Admiral's Walk, and head to the:

15. **Admiral's House.** Built around 1700, this house is notable for its roof, which, in 1791, was adapted to look like a ship's deck by Lt. Fountain North, who lived here from 1775 until his death in 1811. North even installed two cannons, which he fired to celebrate royal birthdays and naval victories. Sir George Gilbert Scott, the architect of Royal Albert Hall, lived here in the late 19th century. The property was immortalized by P. J. Travers as Admiral

Boom's house, Cherry Tree Lane, in the book *Mary Poppins.*

Next door is:

16. **Grove Lodge,** the former home of John Galsworthy (1867–1933), a writer best known for his multivolume *Forsyte Saga.* In 1932, Galsworthy won the Nobel Prize for literature; he was too ill to receive his award in person, so a delegation brought it to him here.

    Continue along Admiral's Walk and turn right onto Lower Terrace. Bear right across the grass triangle to arrive at:

17. **2 Lower Terrace,** a small house that artist John Constable rented during the summers of 1821 and 1822. Constable completed several oil paintings here, including one of Admiral's House and one of the shed in the back garden.

    Facing the house, walk to the right along Lower Terrace, turn left, and cross over Upper Terrace to enter the narrow pathway opposite, called Windmill Hill. Continue ahead to:

18. **Judges' Walk,** a pleasant path with a view that Constable loved. Many of his paintings depict variations of this vista (and some include imaginary houses, a windmill, and even Windsor Castle).

    The Walk takes its name from the Great Plague of 1665, when city magistrates moved their court hearings outdoors to the edge of the heath in order to avoid possible exposure to infection from criminals and their accusers.

    Don't walk on Judges' Walk. Instead, go through the small gap in the iron railing and bear right along the rough pathway. Toward its end, bear left and cautiously cross over West Heath Road. Continue onto Whitestone Walk, where on your right you will see the somewhat dreary:

19. **Whitestone Pond,** named for a nearby white milestone that reads 4 MILES FROM ST. GILES POUNDS; 4½ MILES FROM HOLBORN BARRS. When visiting his friend Leigh Hunt, who lived close by, poet Percy Bysshe Shelley (1792–1822) came to this pond and sailed paper boats with local children.

As you leave Whitestone Walk, go over the pedestrian crossing and turn left. Continue into Spaniards Road and go immediately right through the gap in the rail (a sign points to Vale of Health) to descend the steps onto the rough earth path. You have now arrived at:

20. **Hampstead Heath.** Comprising around 324 hectares (800 acres) of grassy hills and coarse woodlands, criss-crossed by muddy paths and offering stunning views over London, the heath has been a popular day trip for Londoners since the 18th century. As many as 100,000 locals have been known to visit on public holidays.

Continue ahead, bearing right when you arrive at a bench, and then follow the earth path as it descends steeply. Go though the gap in the rail and bear left into the:

21. **Vale of Health.** Until 1777, the area hereabouts was lit-tle more than a malodorous swamp. Over the next few years, however, the marshland was drained and fashion-able housing began to appear. By 1802, this quiet corner of Hampstead was known as the "Vale of Health."

Continue along the unnamed road, and bear right (by the lamppost) into the narrow, atmospheric alleyway that snakes past several residences. Upon reaching the road, go left past the line of houses named "Villas on the Heath," turn left again, and then take the first right. The row of houses immediately on your right is called "Byron Villas." The fourth house down is:

22. **4 Byron Villas,** where author D. H. Lawrence (1885–1930) rented a ground-floor apartment through-out the year of 1915. He and his wife, Freda, intended to form a creative community of like-minded writers in the vicinity. But when his novel *The Rainbow* was denounced as obscene, and duly suppressed, they decided that the only course open to them was to emigrate to America (a plan they never realized). Observing bitterly that "it is the end of my writing for England," Lawrence gave up the flat in December. Contrary to those words, however, he would return to Hampstead in 1923 to live at nearby 1 Elm Row, and his experiences in Hampstead would inspire his short story "The Last Laugh."

Retrace your footsteps to Villas on the Heath and continue along the Vale of Health (you'll see a red mailbox on your right). Keeping to the left, continue past a wild, gorse-covered section of Hampstead Heath. Cross over West Heath Road and continue straight into Squires Mount, pausing by the line of cottages on your left, which are collectively known as:

23. **Squires Mount Croft.** Built in 1704, these are the oldest terrace homes in Hampstead.

Bear right into Cannon Place, where on the left is the clock-topped:

24. **Cannon Hall,** an 18th-century courthouse that was associated with the nearby Lock Up (see stop 25). In the early 20th century, the hall was home to Sir Gerald du Maurier (1873–1934), one of the last great turn-of-the-century actor/managers. Du Maurier made his mark with inspired interpretations of J. M. Barrie's plays and as the original Captain Hook in *Peter Pan.* He was also the father of Dame Daphne du Maurier (1907–1989), author of *Rebecca* and *Jamaica Inn,* who spent several of her childhood years at Cannon Hall.

Return to the corner of Squires Mount. Note the **cannons** for which the hall and place are probably named. At one time, these cannons served as hitching posts. Turn right to descend the steep hill, which changes its name to Cannon Lane. Three quarters of the way down, on the right, is the old:

25. **Parish Lock Up,** 11 Cannon Lane, an 18th-century jailhouse—one of only a few remaining in London. Before the government assumed responsibility for law enforcement, the local Justice of the Peace had this responsibility. This Parish Lock Up was built into the garden wall of Cannon Hall in the 1730s. The single dark cell was a holding pen where prisoners were kept until other arrangements could be made. Soon after the local police force was established in 1829, the jailhouse was moved to the Watchhouse in Holly Walk (see stop 9, p. 156).

At the bottom of the hill, cross Well Road and take the small pathway directly opposite (called Well Passage) to

Well Walk. Turn right at the fountain. A few doors down, on your left, is:

26. **40 Well Walk,** the former home of John Constable. Constable lived here from 1827 until his death 10 years later. The artist's wife, Maria, developed pulmonary consumption soon after their seventh child was born, at the beginning of 1828. A friend who visited shortly before Maria's death recalled that Constable appeared to be his usual self in his wife's presence, but later, when the artist took his guest into another room, Constable burst into tears without speaking. Despite his sorrow, Constable maintained a caustic wit. He once commented to the Hampstead dairyman, "In the future we shall feel obliged if you will send us the milk and the water in separate cans."

Carry on along the left side of Well Walk, continuing over Christchurch Hill. About 1 block down, pause outside:

27. **14 Well Walk,** the home of Marie Carmichael Stopes (1880–1958) during her first and unhappy marriage to Canadian botanist R. R. Gates. A champion of women's rights, Stopes was also an early pioneer of birth control. Her book *Married Love,* written after the annulment of her marriage on the grounds of nonconsummation, became a bestseller. Its appearance helped ease the national moral panic resulting from the high incidence of venereal disease among British soldiers returning from World War I. By advocating sexual enjoyment within marriage, the book was intended to encourage young British men to settle into moral, disease-free, and sexually satisfying unions, while encouraging women to see sex as enjoyable rather than as a duty.

Take the next right onto New End Square and head to:

28. **Burgh House,** New End Square (© 020/7431-0144), a fine Queen Anne–style home from 1703. In 1822, this building was bought by Rev. Allatson Burgh, a minister who was accused of neglecting both his home and his congregation. Eventually, the house came under the control of the Burgh House Trust, which has established a small art gallery and local history museum here. The

house is open Wednesday to Sunday from noon to 5pm. Admission is free.

Retrace your steps to Well Walk and continue straight ahead to Willow Road. Though this is a relatively long walk, much of the route runs along Hampstead Heath, so the scenery is beautiful. Keep to the right side of the road. When you arrive opposite the children's playground, pause outside the easily missed:

29. **2 Willow Road** (© 020/7435-6166). Built in 1939 by architect Erno Goldfinger (1902–87), this is one of Britain's most important examples of Modernist architecture. The building was home to its designer until his death. Acquired by the National Trust in the mid-1990s, the building is filled with furniture (also designed by Goldfinger), plus an art collection that includes works by Henry Moore and Max Ernst. Goldfinger's style was certainly controversial. His critics included Ian Fleming, who is believed to have issued a literary condemnation of the architect by naming his most infamous villain after him!

The house is open to the public by guided tour only from Thursday to Saturday between noon and 4pm. There is an admission charge.

Continue along Willow Road and turn right onto:

30. **Downshire Hill,** one of the most bucolic streets in all Hampstead. Nearly all the homes here are painstakingly preserved 19th-century structures.

Half a block down, on your right, is the:

☕ **Take a Break** **Freemasons Arms,** 32 Downshire Hill, a spacious tavern known for its good lunches and gaming spirit. This is one of the few remaining places in London where skittles is still played. Somewhat like American 10-pin bowling, skittles entails tossing a heavy wooden disk at 9 pins placed 6m (20 ft.) away. Games are held on Tuesday and Saturday nights, and the pub offers a trophy to the "best newcomer."

Exit the pub, turn right, and continue to the pretty church of St. John's Downshire Hill. Turn left to Keats Grove, where 2 blocks ahead, on your right, is:

31. **Keats's House** (Wentworth Place), Keats Grove (© **020/ 7435-2062**), the rather unassuming home where Romantic poet John Keats (1795–1821) lived and worked. The poet, who was very fond of Hampstead, wrote:

> To one who has been long in city pent,
> 'Tis very sweet to look into the fair
> And open face of heaven.

This well-preserved Regency house is now open as a museum, displaying one of Keats's first editions, as well as diaries, letters, assorted memorabilia, and some original furnishings. From April 23 to November 1, the house is open Tuesday to Sunday from noon to 5pm; winter opening days and times vary, so phone ahead for the latest details. There is an admission charge.

Backtrack to St. John's church and bear left to the end of Downshire Hill. Go right onto Rosslyn Hill, which becomes Hampstead High Street, at the end of which, on the right, sits Hampstead Underground Station.

Essentials & Recommended Reading

GETTING AROUND

London can be a difficult city to negotiate. It sometimes seems as though no two streets run parallel to each other, and even locals must regularly consult maps. Construction sites further challenge walkers, but don't be dissuaded from walking: As you'll soon discover with this book, there's really no better way to see London. Remember that, in London, cars have the right-of-way over pedestrians; take care even when the light seems to be in your favor.

It's always best to cross streets at the end of a block in the areas designated for pedestrians (zebra crossings); always look to the *right* for oncoming cars (not to the left).

By Public Transportation

Commuters constantly complain about London's public transport, but visitors find the bus and Tube networks both vast and efficient. Underground stations are abundant, and the red double-decker buses are fun to ride. Both systems are operated by London Regional Transport (LRT), which sets fares based on a zone system—you pay for each zone you cross.

London Regional Transport Travel Information Centres are located in major Underground stations, including Heathrow, King's Cross, Oxford Circus, Piccadilly Circus, and Victoria. Off-hour times vary, but all provide service weekdays from 9am to 5pm. LRT also maintains a 24-hour information service at ℭ **020/7222-1234.**

You can save money by purchasing one of three types of **Travelcards.** A central London 1-day Travelcard is good for unlimited transportation within two zones on the bus and Tube after 9:30am Monday to Friday and all day on weekends and public holidays. For travel at other times, the best value is offered by the Oyster Card, which can be purchased at any London Underground Ticket office. You can buy a seven-day or monthly travel Oyster Card, or a Pre Pay Oyster Card, which allows you to pay as you go and to add more money when necessary. The Oyster Cards are good for travel on the bus, the Underground, and the Docklands Light Railway. You simply touch it on the card readers at Tube and DLR stations and on buses. Full details can be found at Transport for London's website: www.tfl.gov.uk.

By Underground   Londoners depend heavily upon their Underground system—which Americans would call the subway (that word means a pedestrian underpass here)—and locals often call it simply "the Tube." Except for Christmas Day, when the Underground is closed, trains run Monday to Saturday every few minutes from about 5:30am, and Sunday from 7:30am. Closing times vary with each station, but the last trains always leave between 11:30pm and midnight; the last departure time is posted at the entrance of each station. You can buy tickets from station ticket windows or from vending machines. Hold on to your ticket throughout your ride; you must present it when you reach your destination. Also be sure to pick up a handy Tube map, available free at station ticket windows. (There's an Underground map on the inside back cover of this book as well.)

By Bus   On the majority of City Centre buses, you either pay the driver as you enter the bus, or you press your Oyster Card (see above) against the reader as you board. On the long bendy buses, you can board via any door if you have an Oyster Card—simply touch it to the reader as you board. Many bus stops now have ticket machines from which you can purchase your tickets.

Many visitors hesitate to ride the buses because their routes can be quite confusing. Get a free bus map from the tourist office, or just ask any conductor about the route and enjoy a top-deck sightseeing adventure.

As with the Tube, regular bus service stops after midnight. Night buses have different routes and numbers from their daytime counterparts, and service is less frequent. If you've just missed your night bus, expect a long wait for the next; you might prefer to look for a minicab (see below). The central London night-bus terminus is Trafalgar Square. Remember that those handy 1-day Travelcards (see above) aren't valid on night buses; you will need to buy a fare.

By Taxi

For three or four people traveling a short distance, cabs can be economical. The city's big black cabs now come in other colors (primarily maroon), and the ride is still fun. Cabs are designed with a particularly tight turning radius, and there's enough interior room to accommodate a gentleman wearing a top hat. A taxi is available when the yellow sign on its roof is illuminated; hail a cab by raising your arm. The driver (who sits on the right side, this being England) will lower his window when he pulls up to the curb so that you can state your destination before climbing in. You can usually hail a cab on the street or in front of train stations, large hotels, and popular attractions. If you know in advance that you'll need a cab, you can order one by calling © **020/7272-0272.**

Minicabs are meterless cars driven by licensed entrepreneurs. Technically, these taxis aren't allowed to cruise for fares but must operate from sidewalk offices—many of which are located around Leicester Square. Minicabs are handy after the Tube shuts down for the night and black cabs suddenly become scarce. Always negotiate a fare beforehand. If you're ever approached by a lone cab driver who pulls up and simply offers you a ride, a firm but polite "no" is called for; crimes have been committed in this fashion.

By Bicycle

Though there are no bike lanes, and cars are unyielding, some people enjoy biking. If you want to rent a bike, try **On Your Bike,** 52–54 Tooley St., SE1 (*©* **020/7378-6669**), open Monday to Friday from 9am to 6pm, and Saturday from 9:30am to 5:30pm.

By Car

It's not advisable to drive in the city; however, if you're planning some side trips, renting a car is worthwhile. Inexpensive rental companies include **www.easyrentacar.com**, which promises the cheapest rates in London and maintains pickup points at several locations; and **Budget** (*©* **0870/539-170**). Each has several branches throughout the city.

FAST FACTS London

Area Codes The area code for London is **020.** Central London numbers begin with a **7,** and outer London numbers begin with an **8.** Area codes are necessary when dialing from outside the code area. From the United States, first dial the international access code, **011;** then the country code for England, **44;** then 20 (you drop the initial zero when dialing from abroad); followed by the eight-digit local number.

Bookstores **Waterstone's Bookstore,** 82 Gower St., WC1 (*©* **020/7636-1577**), in the heart of the university district, is one of London's largest and best chain bookstores; there are many other locations as well. **Foyles,** 119 Charing Cross Rd., WC2 (*©* **020/7437-5660**), has a vast selection of illogically shelved titles. **Hatchards,** 187 Piccadilly, W1 (*©* **020/7439-9921**), an upscale bookshop, sells popular books and has a good travel section.

Business Hours **Banks** are open Monday to Friday from 9:30am to 4:30pm; many stay open to 5pm, and some are open Saturday from 9:30am to noon. **Stores** are usually open Monday to Saturday from 10am to 6pm, but most stay open at least an additional hour on one evening a week. The stores in Knightsbridge usually remain open to 7pm on Wednesday, and those in the West End stay open late on Thursday. Some shops around touristy Covent Garden stay open to 7 or 8pm every night. Many stores now open on Sundays from 10am to 4pm.

Currency The pound sterling (£), a small, thick, round coin, is divided into 100 pence. Pence, often called simply "p" by the British, come in 1p, 2p, 5p, 10p, and 50p coins. Bills (called "notes" here) are issued in £5, £10, £20, and £50 denominations. Although Britain remains committed to the new euro currency, it has no present schedule for replacing its pound and pence with euros.

Currency Exchange Banks generally offer the best exchange rates, but American Express and Thomas Cook are competitive and don't charge a commission for cashing traveler's checks (even those of other financial institutions). American Express has several offices, including one at 6 Haymarket, SW1 (② **020/7484-9600**), near Trafalgar Square. They are open Monday to Friday from 9am to 6pm and Saturday from 9am to noon. Currency-exchange offices with the longest hours (sometimes open all night) tend to offer the least favorable rates. Beware of Chequepoint and other high-commission change offices.

Embassies The **U.S. Embassy,** 24 Grosvenor Sq., W1 (② **020/7499-9000**), is open to walk-in visitors Monday to Friday from 8:30 to 11am. The **Canadian High Commission,** Macdonald House, 1 Grosvenor Sq., W1 (② **020/7258-6600**), is open Monday to Friday from 9am to 5pm. The **Australian High Commission,** in Australia House on The Strand, WC2 (② **020/7379-4334**), is open Monday to Friday from 9am to 1pm. The **New Zealand High Commission,** in New Zealand House, 80 Haymarket, SW1 (② **020/7930-8422**), is open Monday to Friday from 9am to 5pm.

Emergencies Police, fire, and ambulance services can be reached by dialing ② **999** from any phone. Coins aren't required for these calls.

Holidays Most businesses are closed New Year's Day, Good Friday, Easter Monday, the first Monday in May, and

In London: Best Dining Bets

by Darwin Porter & Danforth Prince

- **Best Spot for a Celebration:** There's no spot in all of London that's more fun than **Quaglino's,** 16 Bury St., SW1 (© **020/7930-6767**), which serves up Continental cuisine. On some nights, as many as 800 diners show up at Sir Terence Conran's gargantuan Mayfair eatery. It's the best place in London to celebrate almost any occasion—and the food's good, too. There's live jazz on Friday and Saturday nights.

- **Best for Value:** Called the market leader in cafe salons, **Veronica's,** 3 Hereford Rd., W2 (© **020/7229-5079**), serves not only some of the best traditional British fare, but also some of the most affordable. Many of the chef's recipes are based on medieval or Tudor culinary secrets.

- **Best Modern British Cuisine:** In a former smokehouse just north of Smithfield Market, **St. John,** 26 St. John St., EC1 (© **020/7251-0848**), serves a modern interpretation of British cuisine like none other in town. The chefs here believe in using offal (those parts of the animal that are usually discarded)—after all, why use just parts of the animal when you can use it all? Although some diners are a bit squeamish at first, they're usually hooked once they get past the first bite. Book ahead of time.

- **Best Traditional British Cuisine:** There is no restaurant in London that's quite as British as **Simpson's-in-the-Strand,** 100 The Strand, WC2 (© **020/7836-9112**), which has been serving the finest English roast beef since 1828. Henry VIII, were he to return, would surely pause for a feast here.

- **Best for Kids:** The owner, the Earl of Bradford, feeds you well and affordably at **Porter's English Restaurant,** 17 Henrietta St., WC2 (© **020/7836-6466**). Kids of all ages dig Lady Bradford's once secretly guarded recipe for banana-and-ginger pudding, along with the most classic English pies served in Central London, including such old-fashioned favorites as lamb and apricot; and ham, leek, and cheese.

- **Best Indian Cuisine:** London's finest Indian food is served at **Café Spice Namaste,** in a landmark Victorian hall near Tower Bridge, 16 Prescot St., E1 (© **020/7488-9242**). You'll be tantalized by an array of spicy southern and northern Indian dishes. We like the cuisine's Portuguese influence; the chef, Cyrus Todiwala, is from Goa (a Portuguese territory absorbed by India).

- **Best Italian Cuisine:** At **Zafferano,** 15 Lowndes St., SW1 (© **020/7235-5800**), master chefs prepare delectable cuisine with ingredients that conjure up the Mediterranean shores. The most refined palates of Knightsbridge come to this chic, rustic trattoria for refined dishes like pheasant and black-truffle ravioli with rosemary.

- **Best Innovative Cuisine:** Irish chef Richard Corrigan brings sophisticated modern British cuisine to **Lindsay House,** 21 Romilly St., W1 (© **020/7439-0450**). The menu depends on what looks good at the daily market combined with the chef's inspiration for the day. When you sample his breast of wood pigeon with foie gras and pumpkin chutney, you'll want to kidnap him for your kitchen.

- **Best for Spotting Celebrities: Archipelago,** 110 Whitfield St., W1 (© **020/7383-3346**), is small and intimate, a cozy retreat for Hugh Hefner and the other celebs in London. Media headliner Michael Von Hruschka runs this Thai and French restaurant with whimsy and many precious touches, such as a drink list inserted in an ostrich eggshell. But the cuisine doesn't depend on gimmicks. It's first rate in both ingredients and preparation.

December 25 and 26. In addition, many stores close on bank holidays, which usually occur on scattered Mondays throughout the year (Good Friday, Christmas Day, Boxing Day, and New Year's Day are also bank holidays). There are no standard holidays for museums, restaurants, or sightseeing attractions. To avoid disappointment, always phone your intended destination before setting out.

Information   The **London Tourist Board (LTB)** staffs several information centers, including one in Victoria Station's forecourt (daily Easter–Oct 8am–7pm and Nov–Easter 9am–6pm).

Mail   Post offices are plentiful and are normally open Monday to Friday from 9am to 5pm and Saturday from 9am to noon. The **Main Post Office,** 24 William IV St., Trafalgar Square, WC2 (✆ **020/7484-9307**), is open Monday to Saturday from 8am to 8pm.

Newspapers/Magazines   There are many local newspapers in London. The indispensable *Time Out* magazine contains comprehensive information on what's happening around the city. There are newsstands outside virtually every Tube station, and a surprisingly good selection of international newspapers and magazines is available at almost any tobacco shop or food market.

Police   In an emergency, dial ✆ **999** from any phone; no coins are needed. At other times, dial the operator at ✆ **100** and ask to be connected with the police.

Taxes   England's 17.5% **value-added tax (VAT)** is already included in the ticket price of most items for sale. International travelers can reclaim the VAT for major purchases; ask at department or specialty stores for details.

Telephone   For details about London's telephone codes, see "Area Codes," above. There are normally two kinds of pay phones: One accepts coins, while the other operates exclusively with phone cards, available from newsstands in £1, £2, £4, £10, and £20 denominations. Phone card telephones automatically deduct the price of your call from the card as you talk. To reach a local operator, dial ✆ **100.** The international operator is reached by dialing ✆ **155.** London information ("directory inquiries") can be reached by dialing ✆ **118-500.** There is a charge for this service.

Tipping   Most (but not all) restaurants automatically add a service charge, noted on the menu. Where a service charge isn't included, a 10% to 15% tip is customary. Note that tipping is rare in pubs.

RECOMMENDED READING

Hundreds, perhaps thousands, of books have been written about London and people who have lived or still live there. From an enormous number of books featuring London, I've chosen those that I believe represent the best.

Writers such as Shakespeare, Dickens, and Anthony Trollope convey ideas of what London was like in earlier periods. Peter Ackroyd's *Dickens's London: An Imaginative Vision* (Headline UK, 1988) is a selection from the fictional and personal writings of one of London's greatest authors, presenting a detailed picture of the city in the early 19th century. Arthur Conan Doyle, creator of fiction's best-loved detective, reveals a colorful, textured view of late-19th-century London in *The Adventures and Memoirs of Sherlock Holmes* (Modern Library, 1946, and many other editions).

Virginia Woolf's *A Room of One's Own,* T. S. Eliot's *The Wasteland,* and George Orwell's *Down and Out in Paris and London* are excellent literary windows into London's more recent past. Evelyn Waugh's *Brideshead Revisited* (Little, Brown, 1982) is set partially abroad and in the counties around London; nevertheless, this magnificent novel describes the London of the early 20th century to a tee. And don't forget the mysteries of Agatha Christie, especially those featuring Belgian super-detective Hercule Poirot.

In *Like to the Lark: The Early Years of Shakespeare* (C. N. Potter, 1972), Frederick Julius Pohl tries to reconstruct Shakespeare's "lost years" in London and attempts to answer many questions about the playwright's life. Dorothy M. George's *London Life in the Eighteenth Century* (Academy Chicago Publishers, 1985) is an enlightened and readable study of London life in the Georgian period. In *Doctor Johnson's London* (Wiley, 1968), Dorothy Marshall re-creates the intellectual, literary, and artistic aspects of the London that Dr. Johnson knew and loved. Richard B. Schwartz's *Daily Life in Johnson's London* (University of Wisconsin Press, 1983) is an acclaimed scholarly study of London—city and society—in the mid–18th century.

In *The London Police in the Nineteenth Century* (Lerner/ Cambridge University Press, 1984), John Wilkes looks at London at the beginning of the Industrial Revolution from a unique perspective. Paul West's *The Women of Whitechapel and Jack the Ripper* (Random House, 1991) is a fictional work that presents rich historical background information as well as actual facts pertaining to the most famous murder case in history.

Twentieth-century London is explored, with a special focus on the Bloomsbury circle of intellectuals and artists, in Jean M. Wilson's *Virginia Woolf, Life and London: A Biography of Place* (Norton, 1988). Stanley Weintraub focuses on the politicking and private lives of American authors and artists who spent considerable time in London before World War I in *The London Yankees: Portraits of American Writers and Artists in England, 1894–1914* (Harcourt Brace, 1979).

London and its social life are also subjects of thousands of general-interest books. *London: A Social History* (Harvard University Press, 1995), by Roy Porter, focuses on the development of London during the past 400 years in light of the interests and commercial activities of its residents. *Long Weekend: A Social History of Great Britain, 1918–1939* (Norton, 1963), by Robert Graves and Alan Hodge, is a fascinating and straightforward account of Britain between the two World Wars. Edward R. Murrow's *This Is London* (Schocken Books, 1989) shows us London during World War II, as seen by the veteran CBS radio news reporter.

In *London: A Concise History* (Scribner's, 1975), Geoffrey Trease examines London's rich and varied past, from the heroic days of the Blitz, through the city's second fire, to the period of reconstruction that followed. Timothy M. Richards guides visitors and history buffs through the many pubs that have played a significant role in London's past in *City of London Pubs: A Practical and Historical Guide* (Drake Publishers, 1973).

The London Encyclopedia (Adler & Adler, 1986), by editors Ben Weinreb and Christopher Hibbert, is the definitive source for in-depth information on thousands of London buildings, institutions, and people. *The Times London History Atlas* (HarperCollins, 1991), by Hugh Clout, contains street and regional maps as well as historical information from London's premier newspaper.

Also Worth the Read

Barker, Felix. *London: 2,000 Years of a City and Its People.* Macmillan, 1974.

Beier, A. L., and Roger Finlay (eds.). *London Fifteen Hundred to Seventeen Hundred: The Making of the Metropolis.* Longman, 1986.

Bennett, Arnold. *London Life.* Ayer, 1976.

Betjeman, John. *Victorian & Edwardian London.* David & Charles, 1969.

Brewster, Dorothy. *Virginia Woolf's London.* Greenwood, 1979.

Brooke, Christopher. *London, 800–1216: The Shaping of a City.* University of California Press, 1975.

Cameron, Robert, and Alistair Cooke. *Above London.* Cameron, 1980.

Chancellor, Edwin B. *The London of Charles Dickens.* Gordon Press, 1976.

Davies, Andrew. *The Map of London: From 1746 to the Present Day.* David & Charles, 1988.

Defoe, Daniel. *Tour Thro' London About the Year 1725.* Ayer, 1929.

Ehrlich, Blake. *London on the Thames.* Little, Brown, 1966.

Ford, Madox. *The Soul of London.* Haskell, 1972.

Gibson-Jarvie, Robert. *The City of London: A Financial & Commercial History.* Longwood Pub. Group, 1979.

Goodard, Donald. *Blimey! Another Book About London.* Quadrangle Books, 1972.

Hibbert, Christopher. *London: The Biography of a City.* Penguin, 1983.

James, Henry. *A London Life.* Arden, 1978.

Jones, Richard. *Walking Haunted London.* New Holland, 1999.

Jones, Richard. *Walking Dickensian London.* New Holland, 2003.

Johnson, Samuel. *Johnson on Johnson: Personal Writings of Samuel Johnson.* Dutton, 1976.

Kirwan, Daniel J. *Palace and Hovel.* Abelard-Schuman, 1963.

Lejeune, Anthony. *The Gentlemen's Clubs of London.* Smith, 1979.

Manley, Lawrence. *London in the Age of Shakespeare.* Pennsylvania State University Press, 1987.

Olsen, Donald J. *The City As a Work of Art: London, Paris, Vienna.* Yale University Press, 1986.

Pepys, Samuel. *Everybody's Pepys: The Diary of Samuel Pepys 1660–1669.* Harcourt Brace, 1926.

Piper, David. *The Artist's London.* Oxford University Press, 1982.

Pritchett, Victor S. *London Perceived.* Harcourt Brace, 1966.

Swinnerton, Frank. *The Bookman's London.* R. West, 1980.

Thompson, John. *Orwell's London.* Schocken, 1985.

Timbs, John. *Clubs & Club Life in London with Anecdotes of Its Famous Coffee-Houses, Hostelries, & Taverns from the Seventeenth Century to the Present Time.* Gale, 1967.

Woolf, Virginia. *The London Scene.* Hallman, 1975.

Index

Shop at the new London's Transport Museum store

Unit 26, Covent Garden Market

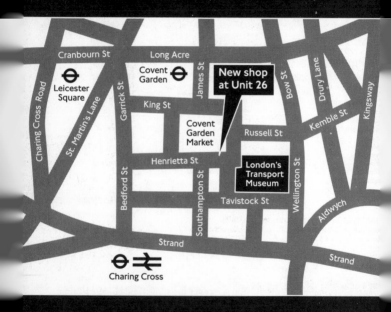

Shop online at **www.ltmuseum.co.uk**

Store open daily: **10.00 – 18.00** (Closed 25 and 26 December)

London's Transport Museum is closed for refurbishment until 2007

FROMMER'S® DOLLAR-A-DAY GUIDES

FROMMER'S® PORTABLE GUIDES

FROMMER'S® CRUISE GUIDES